PUZZLE IT!
MATH COMPUTATION PUZZLES

by Jessica J. Krattinger

Designed & Illustrated
by Kathleen Bullock

Incentive Publications
Nashville, Tennessee

Cover by Angela Stiff
Edited by Marjorie Frank and Jill Norris
Copy edited by Cary Grayson and Steve Carlon

ISBN 978-0-86530-514-4

1   2   3   4   5   6   7   8   9   10   10   09   08   07

PRINTED IN THE UNITED STATES OF AMERICA
www.incentivepublications.com

CONTENTS

WELCOME

TO THE FUN OF MATH COMPUTATION PUZZLES

Everybody loves a puzzle! A puzzle is like an unsolved mystery, teasing you to be the one that unravels it. There are few things that match the feeling of satisfaction you experience when, after thinking long and hard about a puzzle, the solution suddenly materializes—clear as crystal. It is a truly magical moment, one that will be remembered.

Here's some more magic: When students wrestle with a puzzle, classroom learning is energized. Who can walk away from the invitation to tackle a puzzle? It's too much fun to try to figure it out. Even the most reluctant students seem to wake up and be drawn into the solution process. But puzzles are much more than fun! They give the brain a workout and nurture problem-solving skills.

Every classroom and home should offer many puzzle-solving opportunities. The National Council of Teachers of Mathematics identifies problem solving as "the cornerstone of school mathematics." The critical thinking and problem-solving skills that are honed while solving puzzles are basic. They apply to every facet and subject area of learning. In solving puzzles, students make use of such thinking skills as logic, analysis, synthesis, sequencing, creativity, induction, and deduction—and they often must use several of these simultaneously! They must observe, ask questions, consider strategies, try different strategies, visualize different possibilities, and figure out why one thing works and another does not. Many puzzles also refine hand-eye or hand-mind coordination, spatial awareness, and mental gymnastics.

Puzzles must be a part of every serious curriculum. The puzzles in the **Puzzle It!** series challenge students to analyze information and use their critical thinking skills.

ABOUT THE PUZZLES IN THIS BOOK

All of these puzzles sharpen skills in math computation. Starting with addition, they progress to all operations with whole numbers, fractions, decimals, exponential numbers, and positive and negative numbers.

Find missing numbers, practice your computation, check answers, and solve equations as you crack codes, color hidden pictures, follow trails, find your way through mazes, play Bingo, locate mystery numbers, and untangle many other delightful puzzles. The puzzles make heavy use of graphic and other visual clues, and often require you to color or draw. So keep your markers and crayons handy.

How To Use The Puzzles

• Look over each puzzle carefully. Read the instructions a few times.

• Consider the puzzle thoughtfully. Make sure the purpose of the puzzle is clear to you.

• Evaluate what it is you must figure out or find.

• Experiment with different strategies and different ideas. Try out different solutions.

• Take one puzzle at a time. A puzzle will grab you and won't let go until you figure it out. So let it swirl around in your head—even over a few days. Stay with it until you reach a solution.

• Try not to peek at the answers. Ask someone else for an idea or a hint if you need help.

• You can tackle a puzzle alone, or share a puzzle with one or more friends, and tackle it together. Share ideas, discuss, argue—until you arrive at a solution.

• When you find a solution, discuss it with someone else. Explain the steps and strategies you used to reach your answer. Compare your solution and methods with someone else's.

About The Solutions . . .

Answers are given for all the puzzles. However, sometimes a puzzle has more than one solution. Give yourself or your students credit for any solution that can be reasonably explained.

Since a main purpose of these puzzles is to sharpen your calculation skills, it is advisable to leave your calculator turned off while you solve the problems. If you want practice with your calculator, use it to check your answers.

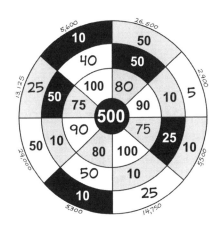

A Case Of Missing Addends

The tiles on the floor are the clues Detective C.C. Sly needs to solve the mystery of the lost addends. Help him find the missing digits.

Directions:

Some parts of the puzzle are blank. Find the missing numbers.
The sum of numbers in connected white squares in vertical or horizontal rows must equal 12.

Here's a clue that will help:
A square may have a two-digit number.

Name_____

CARD PUZZLER

Knowing the sums will help you solve the puzzle of the hidden cards.

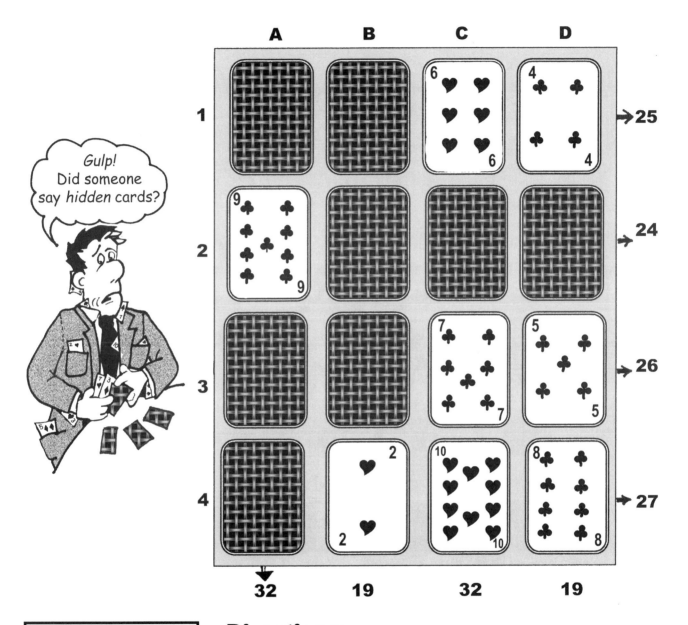

Directions:

There are eight pairs of cards in the diagram. Each pair consists of a heart card and a club card with the same number. (For example, the 4 of hearts and the 4 of clubs are a pair.)

The sums of the four cards in each column and row are shown. Figure out what the unseen cards are. Write a description of each card (for example, "7 of hearts") in the answer box.

A-1 is _____

A-3 is _____

A-4 is _____

B-1 is _____

B-2 is _____

B-3 is _____

C-2 is _____

D-2 is _____

CAUGHT IN THE WEB

This sticky web catches many things. Find out what and where they are!

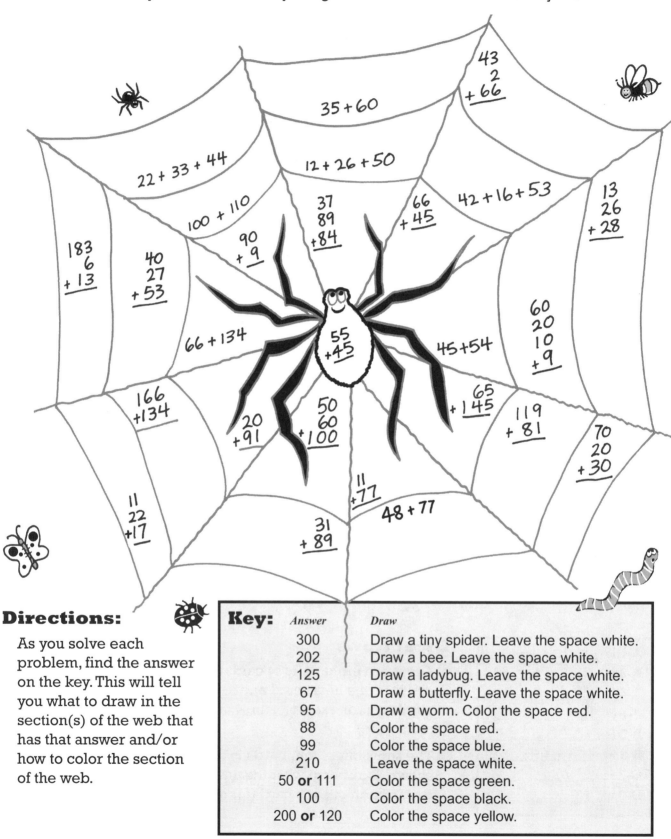

Directions:

As you solve each problem, find the answer on the key. This will tell you what to draw in the section(s) of the web that has that answer and/or how to color the section of the web.

Key:

Answer	Draw
300	Draw a tiny spider. Leave the space white.
202	Draw a bee. Leave the space white.
125	Draw a ladybug. Leave the space white.
67	Draw a butterfly. Leave the space white.
95	Draw a worm. Color the space red.
88	Color the space red.
99	Color the space blue.
210	Leave the space white.
50 **or** 111	Color the space green.
100	Color the space black.
200 **or** 120	Color the space yellow.

Name_____

STRAIGHT FROM THE HONEYCOMB

The bees may know the missing numbers, but you'll need to figure them out!

Directions:

The honeycomb (when finished) will contain the digits **1-19.** All the rows (shown by the arrows) must add up to **38.** Fill in the missing numbers.

Name_____

SOMETHING'S DANCING

The music is playing and it's just right for dancing. Find the dancer!

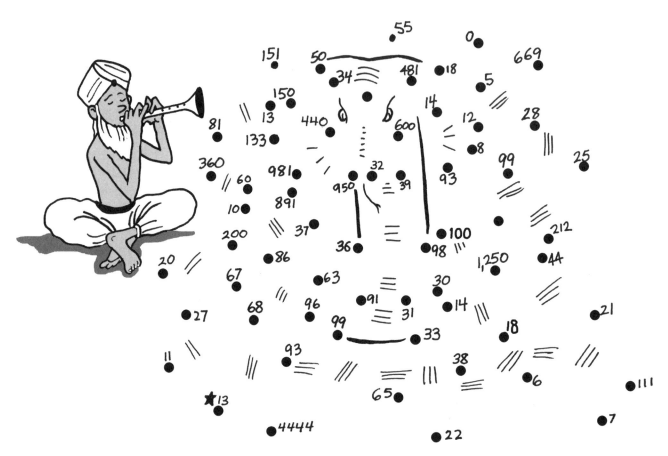

Directions:

Solve the first problem. Find that answer on the puzzle. Draw a line from the star to the dot beside that answer. Solve the next problem. Look for the answer in the puzzle. Connect the dots. Keep connecting the dots in order as you solve the problems.

1. $476 - \rule{1cm}{0.15mm} = 408$

2. $219 - \rule{1cm}{0.15mm} = 120$

3. $432 - 396 = \rule{1cm}{0.15mm}$

4. $\rule{1cm}{0.15mm} - 711 = 270$

5. $1,000 - \rule{1cm}{0.15mm} = 850$

6. $442 - \rule{1cm}{0.15mm} = 392$

7. $958 - \rule{1cm}{0.15mm} = 924$

8. $2,462 - \rule{1cm}{0.15mm} = 2,022$

9. $1,826 - 876 = \rule{1cm}{0.15mm}$

10. $697 - \rule{1cm}{0.15mm} = 665$

11. $795 - 195 = \rule{1cm}{0.15mm}$

12. $594 - 113 = \rule{1cm}{0.15mm}$

13. $303 - \rule{1cm}{0.15mm} = 285$

14. $2,200 - \rule{1cm}{0.15mm} = 2,192$

15. $194 - \rule{1cm}{0.15mm} = 96$

16. $689 - \rule{1cm}{0.15mm} = 656$

17. $93 - \rule{1cm}{0.15mm} = 75$

18. $621 - \rule{1cm}{0.15mm} = 600$

19. $426 - \rule{1cm}{0.15mm} = 315$

20. $186 - \rule{1cm}{0.15mm} = 179$

21. $66 - \rule{1cm}{0.15mm} = 44$

22. $9,876 - 5,432 = \rule{1cm}{0.15mm}$

23. $27 - \rule{1cm}{0.15mm} = 14$

Name_____

MYSTERY HOOPS

Solve the mystery of each hoop, and it will be easy to find the missing numbers.

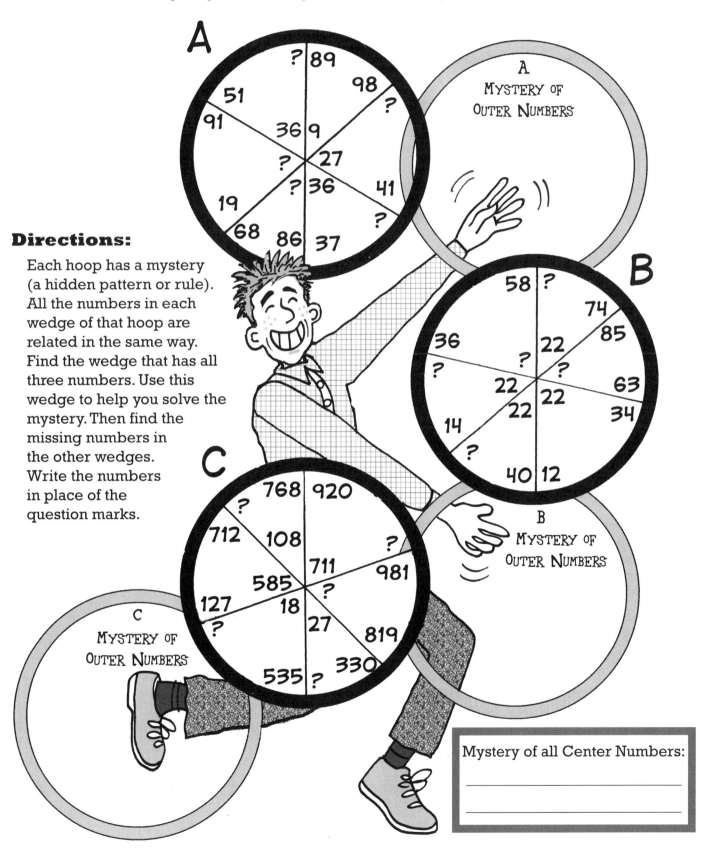

A

? | 89
51
98
91 | ?
36 | 9
? | 27
? | 36
19
68 | 86 | 37
41
?

A
MYSTERY OF
OUTER NUMBERS

B

58 | ?
74
36
85
? | 22
?
? | 22 | ?
14 | 22 | 22 | 63
? | 34
40 | 12

B
MYSTERY OF
OUTER NUMBERS

Directions:

Each hoop has a mystery (a hidden pattern or rule). All the numbers in each wedge of that hoop are related in the same way. Find the wedge that has all three numbers. Use this wedge to help you solve the mystery. Then find the missing numbers in the other wedges. Write the numbers in place of the question marks.

C

768 | 920
?
712 | 108
?
711
585 | 981
?
127 | 18
27
?
535 | ? | 330
819

C
MYSTERY OF
OUTER NUMBERS

Mystery of all Center Numbers:

_____

_____

Puzzle It! Math Computation Puzzles

TAKE NOTE

There's a tune in the air. Complete the musical puzzle
to figure out what it is.

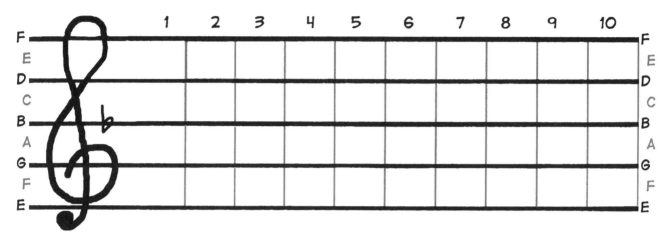

Directions:

Each problem corresponds to a section on the musical score.

After you solve each problem, look at the answer.
Follow the KEY to find out what kind of note you should draw.

Draw the note in the correct spot. Draw notes for low E, G, B, D, and high F on the lines.
Draw notes for low F, A, C, and high E in the spaces.

Note Location:	Problem:
Section 1, low F	$312 - 282 =$
Section 2, low F	$10,000 - 9,974 =$
Section 3, low F	$151 - 76 =$
Section 4, G	$361 - 88 =$
Section 5, A	$237 - 189 =$
Section 6, A	$3,917 - 1,708 =$
Section 7, G	$1,101 - 100 =$
Section 8, A	$682 - 91 =$
Section 9, B	$895 - 478 =$
Section 10, C	$890 - 718 =$

NOTES TO DRAW:

- if the answer is an even number > 50.

- if the answer is an even number < 50.

- if the answer is an odd number.

NAME THAT TUNE!

?

Look at the notes you have written. Try to hum the tune. Can you Identify it?

THE AMAZING 4

Only **FOUR** will open the door. If your answer has a four in it, you are on the right path!

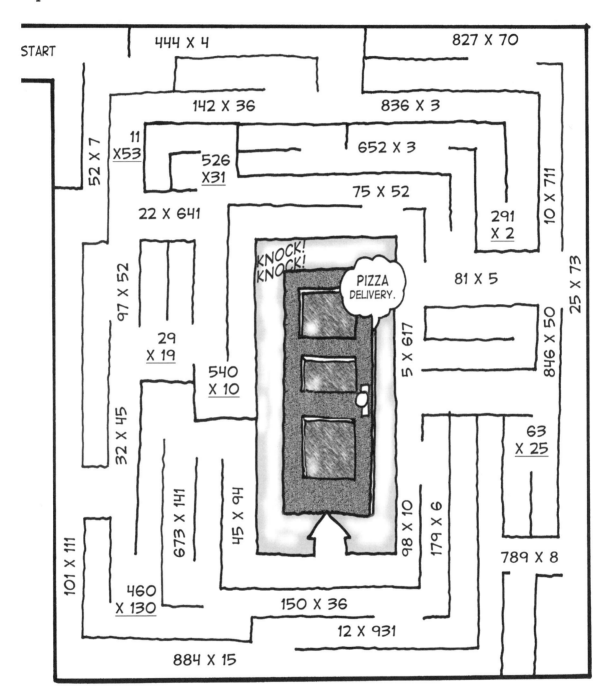

Directions:

Begin at **Start**. As you travel along the maze, solve each problem. If the answer has a 4 in it, keep moving in that direction. If the answer does NOT have a 4, you will need to try a different route. Keep following the problems with "4-ish" answers until you get the delivery to the DOOR!

Name_____

FRANTIC ANTICS

The red ants will solve the puzzle. But watch out, they sting!

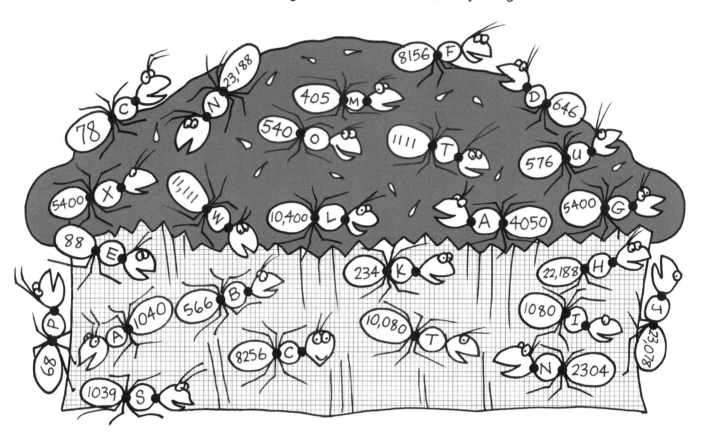

Directions:

Solve each problem. Find an ant with the answer. Color that ant red. Unscramble the letters on the red ants to find the answer to the riddle below.

1. 13 x 6 =

2. 12 x 45 =

3. 75 x 54 =

4. 101 x 11 =

5. 8 x 72 =

6. 65 x 16 =

7. 288 x 8 =

8. 344 x 24 =

9. 682 x 34 =

10. 504 x 20 =

What kind of insect can help you with your budget or your income tax?

____ ____ ____ ____ ____ ____ ____ ____ ____

Name_____

TREASURE MAP NUMBERS

It will take sharp multiplication skills to track down the numbers leading to buried treasure and other pirate paraphernalia.

Find my doubloons!

1	2	3 -C	4	5 -X	6	6
7	8	9	10	1	2	2
3 -A	4	5	20	9	8	7 -P
1	6	9	4	7	6	5
5	4	3	2	1	0	12
11	12	10	9	8	7	6
6 -Q	5	4 -B	21	10 -Z	22	1 -D

Directions: Draw . . .

a **red line** from **A** to **B**, connecting numbers with a product of **8,640** dry bones.

a **black line** from **C** to **D** connecting numbers with a product of **47,040** wooden legs.

a **blue line** from **P** to **Q** connecting numbers with a product of **0** rusty hooks.

a **green line** from **X** to **Z** connecting numbers with a product of **360,000** silver doubloons.

Note:

All lines must join numbers that are contiguous (horizontally, vertically, or diagonally). Do not skip any rows or columns when joining numbers. Multiply the numbers as you follow the line. This will lead you to a final product for each path.

Name_____

NEVER, EVER SMILE AT ONE

Just pack your stuff and start to run! (Solve the puzzle to see what it is!)

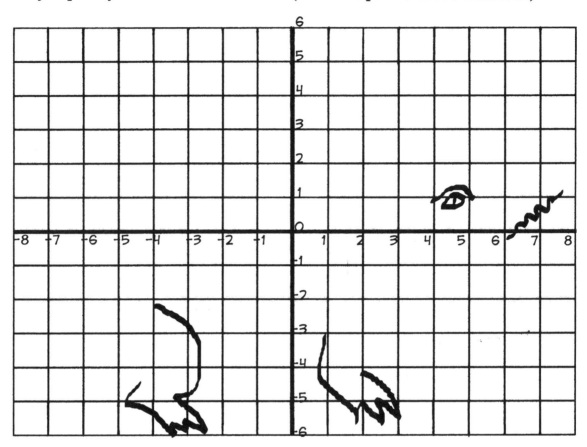

Directions:

Find the missing number to solve each problem.

When you get an answer, find it on the KEY. The key will give you a location on the coordinate grid. Draw a black point at that location.

Connect the points in the order of the problems.

1) ___ x 15 = 105

2) 3 x ___ = 39

3) 11 x 2 = ___

4) 66 x ___ = 0

5) ___ x 11 = 121

6) ___ x 66 = 198

7) 40 x ___ = 600

8) ___ x 12 = 360

9) 75 x ___ = 750

10) 330 = 55 x ___

11) 26 x ___ = 520

12) 2 x ___ = 88

13) ___ x 25 = 100

14) ___ x 12 = 144

15) 4 x ___ = 56

16) ___ x 500 = 2,500

17) 1000 = 40 x ___

18) ___ x 22 = 176

19) ___ x 50 = 800

20) 21 x ___ = 189

21) ___ x 30 = 210

KEY

0 = (–7, –2)	12 = (4, 0)
3 = (–2, –4)	13 = (–6, 4)
4 = (8, 2)	14 = (2, –1)
5 = (–2, 0)	15 = (0, –4)
6 = (5, –2)	16 = (–6, 2)
7 = (–5, 5)	20 = (8, –1)
8 = (–6, 0)	22 = (–8, 1)
9 = (–5, 4)	25 = (–5, –1)
10 = (3, –3)	30 = (2, –4)
11 = (–5, –4)	44 = (5, –1)

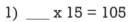

Name_____

AFTER-DINNER MATH

Use your calculation skills to discover the end to the after-dinner conversation.

WHAT DID THE MATHEMATICIAN SAY TO THE WAITER?

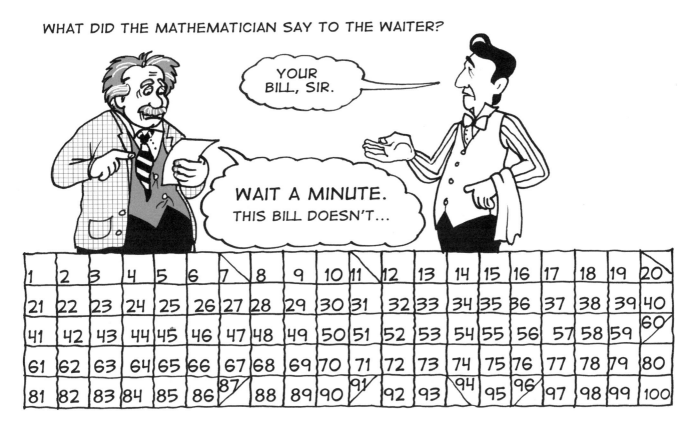

Directions:

Solve each problem. Find the square on the grid that has the answer. Color the whole square or half (diagonal) of the square that contains the answer. When you are finished, the grid will show you what the mathematician said.

1–49: Color the entire square.

1. 320 ÷ 8 =
2. 70 ÷ 5 =
3. 410 ÷ 10 =
4. 90 ÷ 30 =
5. 231 ÷ 11 =
6. 21 x 3 =
7. 76 ÷ 2 =
8. 3 x 14 =
9. 216 ÷ 4 =
10. 402 ÷ 67 =
11. 7 x 7 =
12. 145 ÷ 5 =
13. 188 ÷ 4 =
14. 4 x 14 =
15. 76 ÷ 38 =
16. 3 x 12 =
17. 144 ÷ 9 =
18. 90 ÷ 2 =
19. 4 x 19 =
20. 184 ÷ 8 =
21. 260 ÷ 4 =
22. 415 ÷ 5 =
23. 400 ÷ 80 =
24. 162 ÷ 6 =
25. 26 x 3 =
26. 100 ÷ 100 =
27. 134 ÷ 2 =
28. 198 ÷ 11 =
29. 305 ÷ 5 =
30. 2 x 37 =
31. 430 ÷ 10 =
32. 575 ÷ 23 =
33. 5 x 17 =
34. 144 ÷ 16 =
35. 29 x 2 =
36. 1,710 ÷ 90 =
37. 3 x 23 =
38. 177 ÷ 3 =
39. 729 ÷ 9 =
40. 2 x 17 =
41. 356 ÷ 4 =
42. 5 x 19 =
43. 213 ÷ 3 =
44. 7,380 ÷ 82 =
45. 372 ÷ 12 =
46. 306 ÷ 6 =
47. 196 ÷ 2 =
48. 430 ÷ 5 =
49. 400 ÷ 40 =

50–57: Color the half of the square that contains the answer.

50. 100 ÷ 5 =
51. 84 ÷ 12 =
52. 66 ÷ 6 =
53. 174 ÷ 2 =
54. 5 x 12 =
55. 16 x 6 =
56. 182 ÷ 2 =
57. 564 ÷ 6 =

Name_____

BITE INTO BINGO

Practice division while you play a tasty game of Bingo.

Directions:

Get some coins, buttons, or stones to use as Bingo markers.

Solve each division problem. Find the remainder on the KEY. The key will tell you which Bingo square to mark. Place a marker on that square. You can call, "Bingo!" when all the squares in any row are marked. (The row can be horizontal, vertical, or diagonal. A diagonal row must pass through the center.)
The center square is a free square.

1. $172 \div 21 =$
2. $798 \div 86 =$
3. $382 \div 46 =$
4. $375 \div 26 =$
5. $205 \div 24 =$
6. $597 \div 83 =$

7. $446 \div 74 =$
8. $822 \div 18 =$
9. $1000 \div 99 =$
10. $890 \div 58 =$
11. $305 \div 25 =$
12. $288 \div 41 =$

KEY

Remainder	Bingo Square
1	G, ice cream cone
2	I, hot dog
3	B, watermelon
4	O, cookie
5	G, pineapple
6	O, popcorn
7	B, grapes
8	N, ice cream cone
9	O, cupcake
10	B, pizza
11	I, milkshake
12	N, cupcake
13	O, pizza
14	B, popcorn
15	I, taco
16	G, apple
17	B, cupcake
18	I, cookie
19	G, banana
20	N, taco
21	G, watermelon
22	I, apple
23	O, hot dog
24	N, banana

Name_____

DIAL UP A PUZZLE

Turn your phone into a puzzle-solver. Translate the words into numbers.

Directions:

Find the number for each letter. Write these beneath the letters. In each problem below, find the sum of all the numbers to the left of the division sign. Divide that number by the sum of the numbers in the divisor. Show the remainders.

Example:

BYE + HI
2 + 9 + 3   4 + 4

$14 \div 8 = 1, R 6$

1. PHONE ÷ CALL =

2. OPERATOR ÷ GO =

3. CAN YOU HEAR ME ÷ NOW? =

4. WHO'S ON THE LINE? ÷ NO ONE =

5. DON'T ANSWER THAT! ÷ WHY NOT? =

6. YOUR CELL PHONE BILL IS OUTRAGEOUS! ÷ REALLY? =

7. Make up one of your own!

Name_____

A STRANGE LAW

Solve this coded puzzle to learn about an unusual old law in Omaha, Nebraska.

In Omaha, an old law prohibits

$$\overline{13}\ \overline{8}\ \overline{2}\ \overline{9}\ \overline{14}\ \overline{22}\ \overline{17}$$

$$\overline{6}\ \overline{12}$$

$$\overline{7}\ \overline{15}\ \overline{4}\ \overline{10}\ \overline{21}\ \overline{5}\ \overline{18}\ \overline{1}$$

$$\overline{25}\ \overline{16}$$

$$\overline{20}\ \overline{24}\ \overline{19}\ \overline{11}\ \overline{23}\ \overline{3}$$

Alphabet Key

A = 27
B = 3
C = 41
D = 44
E = 99
G = 45
H = 185
I = 30
L = 101
N = 56
O = 9
P = 79
R = 63
S = 71
T = 69
U = 98
W = 305
Y = 16
Z = 31

Directions:

Solve the problems. Each numerical answer is the code number that matches a letter. Find the number on the Alphabet Key. Write the matching letter on the line above the problem number. This will reveal the details of a surprising law.

That's a law?

1. 225 ÷ 5 =
2. 315 ÷ 5 =
3. 6105 ÷ 33 =
4. 594 ÷ 6 =
5. 450 ÷ 15 =
6. 99 ÷ 11 =
7. 426 ÷ 6 =
8. 1078 ÷ 11 =

9. 1659 ÷ 21 =
10. 792 ÷ 8 =
11. 756 ÷ 12 =
12. 945 ÷ 15 =
13. 267 ÷ 89 =
14. 510 ÷ 17 =
15. 504 ÷ 9 =
16. 616 ÷ 11 =
17. 2250 ÷ 50 =

18. 672 ÷ 12 =
19. 588 ÷ 6 =
20. 902 ÷ 22 =
21. 775 ÷ 25 =
22. 168 ÷ 3 =
23. 4551 ÷ 111 =
24. 1110 ÷ 6 =
25. 810 ÷ 27 =

Name_____

DOMINO ADDITION

Use the spots on dominoes to show off your mental computation skills.

I'm here to connect the dots!

Directions:

Use mental math to figure out these answers.

1. What is the sum of all the ends (domino sections that do not touch another domino at the end)?

2. Circle the individual domino that has the greatest sum. (Add all the dots on the domino piece.)

3. What straight line in the puzzle has the greatest product? (Multiply together all the amounts in the line.)

4. Find a horizontal line-up of six single frames. What is the sum of all amounts?

5. Circle a line of dominoes (horizontal or vertical) that has a product of 108.

Name_____

NUMBER JUMBLE

Solve the problems by pulling numbers from the puzzle. But watch out!
Some numbers that you need are missing.

Directions:

A. Solve the problems. Find the digits on the puzzle to form your answers.

If your answer has the same digit more than once, you must find that digit more than once in the puzzle. (For instance, if the answer is 777, you would have to find three sevens. You can't form the number because the puzzle only has two sevens.)

B. Name the numbers that should replace the question marks in the puzzle.

1. the largest 3-digit number that is a multiple of six

2. the product of 37 and 71

3. a number that is 326 more than 774

4. the smallest number that can be made with the digits 8, 4, 0, and 1

5. the difference between 33,333 and 6,666

6. the largest 4-digit number possible that has all odd digits (All the digits are different.)

7. the largest 3-digit multiple of 5 that has no zeros

8. the largest 4-digit number possible that contains a zero

9. the sum of 111 and 222

10. the quotient in this problem: $10,506 \div 102 =$

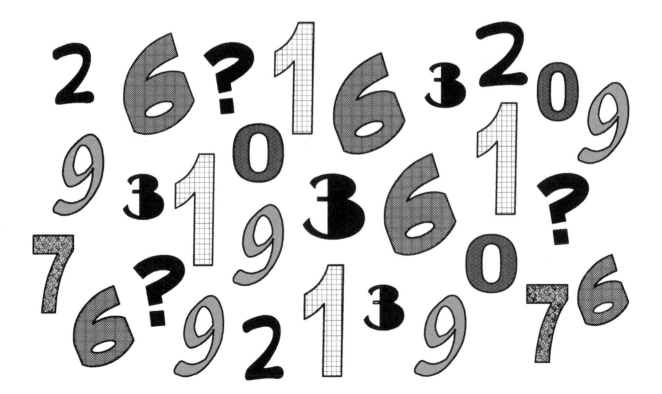

A PUZZLING PAINTING

Painter Seymour B. Rushes has done a good job of painting a huge crossword on the classroom wall. Now he needs help with some calculations that will solve the puzzle.

Directions:

Use the clue to find each number.

Across		
		27. 8 + 11 =
1. 156 x 4 =	15. 273 ÷ 21 =	28. 666 − 589 =
4. 20 x 163 =	16. 31 − 19 =	29. 2222 x 4 =
8. 1000 − 293 =	18. 17 + 33 =	31. 44 ÷ 1 =
10. 92,000 ÷ 9,200 =	19. 1100 ÷ 100 =	32. 5 x 114 =
12. 55 + 25 =	21. 350 − 260 =	33. 396 ÷ 12 =
13. 45,000 ÷ 5 =	23. 28 + 33 =	35. 25 x 6 =
14. 200 − 101 =	25. 3 x 9 =	36. 25 x 40 =

Down		
2. 100 − 73 =	11. 5 x 158 =	24. 750 + 794 =
3. 1166 + 2927 =	15. 512 + 510 =	26. 10 x 787 =
5. 1001 + 1100 =	17. 4000 − 1001 =	27. 305 x 6 =
6. 5400 ÷ 90 =	19. 2 x 2 x 2 x 2 =	30. 400,000 ÷ 5000 =
7. 1000 − 14 =	20. 121 ÷ 11 =	32. 11 x 5 =
9. 2 x 35 =	22. 1635 + 844 =	34. 2010 − 1980 =

Name_____

BUG BOGGLE

Bug names are hiding in the grid. How many can you find?

	A	B	C	D	E	F	G	H
1								
2								
3								
4								
5								

Directions:

1. Solve the problems on the next page. Notice that each problem is connected to a particular grid location. (A-1 is the space under the A column and the first row.)

2. For each problem, find the answer on the ALPHABET KEY.

3. Write the corresponding letter in the correct grid square.

4. When the grid is complete, you will have formed a Word-Find Puzzle.

5. Use the puzzle to find the names of bugs. Find at least six. Draw a line to connect the letters of a name.

These puzzles drive me buggy!

Rule:

The letters must be contiguous—above, below, beside, or diagonal from each other. You may spell the word moving ANY direction from each letter.

Name_____

BUG BOGGLE, CONTINUED

6. Draw a picture of each bug you found on the puzzle (previous page). Label the bug with its name for the bug gallery.

bug gallery

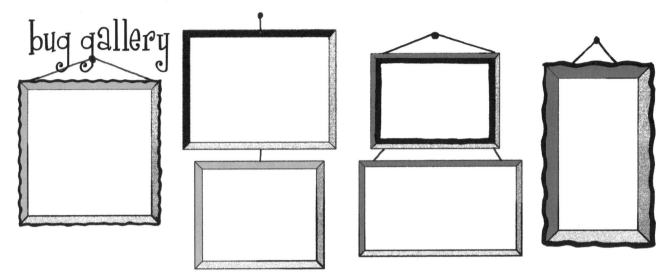

Solve the problems.

Location	Problem	Answer		Location	Problem	Answer
A–1	330 – 27	= _____		E–1	3 x 101	= _____
A–2	72 + 19 + 9	= _____		E–2	1188 ÷ 66	= _____
A–3	636 ÷ 6	= _____		E–3	174 ÷ 6	= _____
A–4	200 ÷ 5	= _____		E–4	1910 – 1870	= _____
A–5	321 + 345	= _____		E–5	1515 ÷ 5	= _____
B–1	935 – 895	= _____		F–1	75,000 ÷ 1500	= _____
B–2	424 ÷ 4	= _____		F–2	330 – 27	= _____
B–3	1000 – 944	= _____		F–3	(3 x 12) + 14	= _____
B–4	(3 x 20) – 10	= _____		F–4	(40 x 25) – 100	= _____
B–5	84,000 ÷ 2100	= _____		F–5	456 + 444	= _____
C–1	276 ÷ 23	= _____		G–1	1056 ÷ 88	= _____
C–2	40 x 2	= _____		G–2	100 – 15	= _____
C–3	45,000 ÷ 50	= _____		G–3	14 x 4	= _____
C–4	713 – 685	= _____		G–4	77 + 236	= _____
C–5	12 + 8 – 3	= _____		G–5	912 ÷ 76	= _____
D–1	3 x 3 + 16	= _____		H–1	110 – 81	= _____
D–2	887 + 13	= _____		H–2	2 x 4 x 5	= _____
D–3	2000 ÷ 40	= _____		H–3	222 – 194	= _____
D–4	(9 x 33) + 16	= _____		H–4	264 ÷ 4	= _____
D–5	11 x 2 x 3	= _____		H–5	5 x 20 x 10	= _____

ALPHABET KEY

40 = A	
80 = B	
95 = C	
12 = D	
900 = E	
18 = F	
56 = G	
55 = H	
1000 = I	
100 = J	
10 = K	
303 = L	
78 = M	
50 = N	
85 = O	
66 = P	
90 = Q	
29 = R	
28 = S	
313 = T	
106 = U	
17 = V	
666 = W	
19 = X	
25 = Y	
15 = Z	

Name_____

A STAR-CROSSED PUZZLE

Add up every line that crosses the star . . . and find the magic number!

Directions:

Every row of numbers in the star has the same sum. This sum is the "magic number" for this magic star. There are six sums to find. Fill in the missing numbers.

What is the magic number? _____

Name_____

SIDEWALK CHALLENGE

Sasha and Sam are the fastest, steadiest, trickiest skateboarders in the neighborhood; but Twister Alley might trip them up.

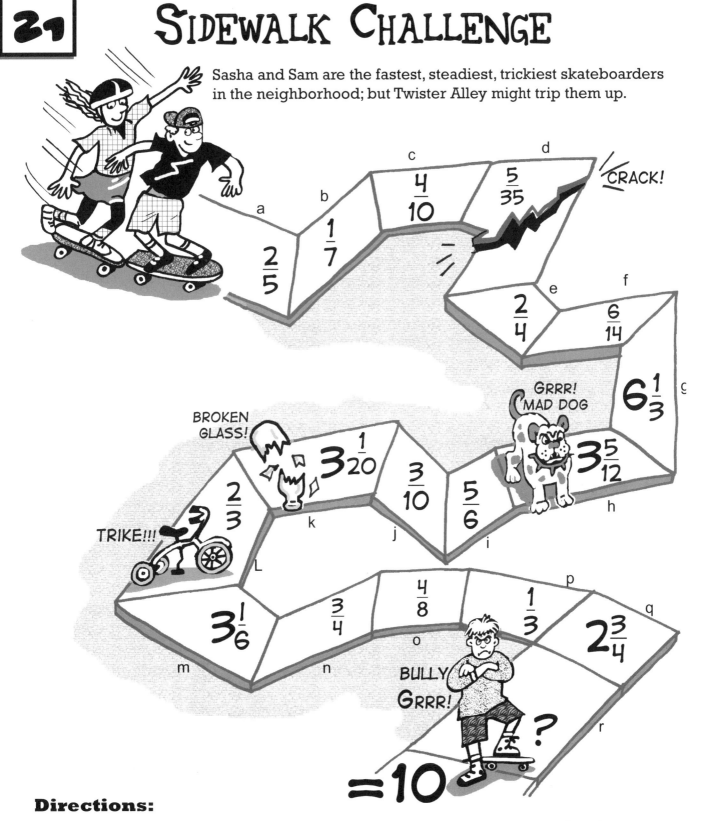

Directions:

As the skateboarders cruise along Twister Alley they **add** up the value of each sidewalk section. However, when they come to a section with an obstruction, they must leap over it or maneuver around it and **subtract** the value of that section. When they get to the end of Twister Alley, they will have a total of 10. But what is the missing value? Fill in the right number on that last obstruction.

Name_____

THE SPIN CYCLE

The spinner on the cycle can help you find missing addends, sums, and differences.

Directions:

One spin of the spinner (or maybe two) can solve each of the problems.

One Spin: Assume there is one spin. What would it have to be to solve each problem? Fill in the missing fraction. (Do not use a fraction from the wheel more than once.)

1. $\frac{1}{4} + \boxed{} = \frac{5}{8}$

2. $\boxed{} - \frac{7}{8} = \frac{11}{8}$

3. $\frac{1}{3} + \frac{5}{9} = \boxed{}$

4. $\boxed{} + \frac{20}{24} = 6$

5. $\frac{3}{4} - \frac{2}{8} = \boxed{}$

6. $\frac{10}{12} - \frac{17}{24} = \boxed{}$

7. $\frac{7}{9} - \boxed{} = \frac{1}{9}$

8. $\boxed{} + \frac{1}{4} = \frac{18}{50}$

9. $\frac{13}{15} - \frac{7}{60} = \boxed{}$

Two OR MORE Spins: Assume there are two or three spins. What would the results have to be to solve these? Write the missing numbers.

10. $\boxed{} - \boxed{} = \frac{8}{49}$

11. $\boxed{} + \boxed{} = \frac{17}{18}$

12. $\boxed{} + \boxed{} + \boxed{} = 1\frac{9}{11}$

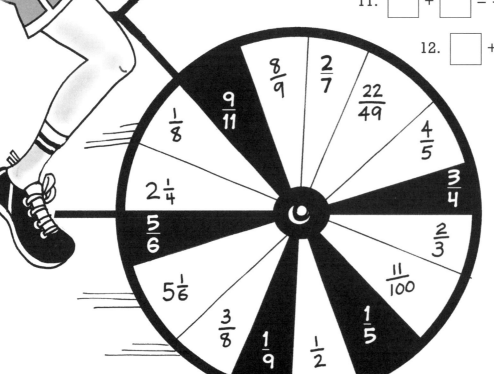

Name_____

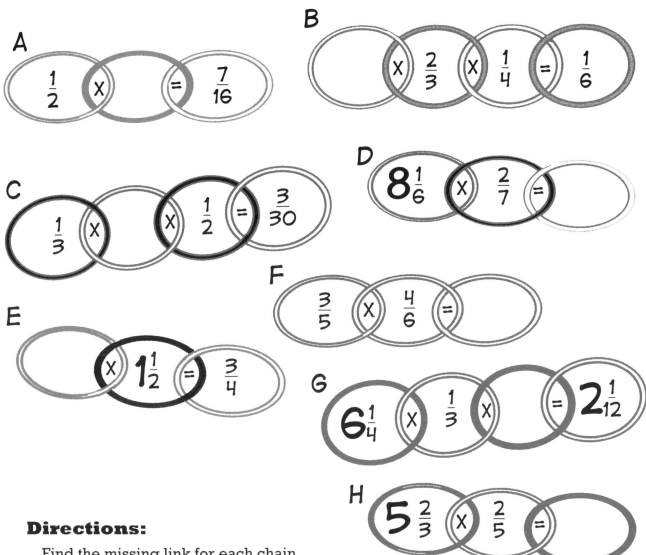

MISSING LINKS

Each chain holds a multiplication problem, but missing links obscure the solution.

A $\frac{1}{2}$ (x) ( ) (=) $\frac{7}{16}$

B ( ) (x) $\frac{2}{3}$ (x) $\frac{1}{4}$ (=) $\frac{1}{6}$

C $\frac{1}{3}$ (x) ( ) (x) $\frac{1}{2}$ (=) $\frac{3}{30}$

D $8\frac{1}{6}$ (x) $\frac{2}{7}$ (=) ( )

E ( ) (x) $1\frac{1}{2}$ (=) $\frac{3}{4}$

F $\frac{3}{5}$ (x) $\frac{4}{6}$ (=) ( )

G $6\frac{1}{4}$ (x) $\frac{1}{3}$ (x) ( ) (=) $2\frac{1}{12}$

H $5\frac{2}{3}$ (x) $\frac{2}{5}$ (=) ( )

Directions:

Find the missing link for each chain. Then solve the puzzle below by writing the missing numbers in the links in order from least to greatest.

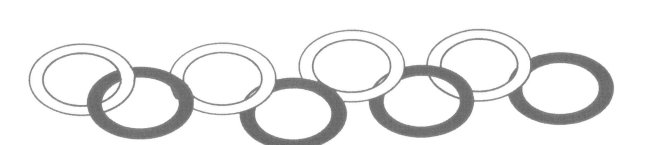

Name_____

PUT IT INTO WORDS

There are numbers in this cross-number puzzle, but you have to spell them out!

Doing math is nine-tenths mental. The other half is practice, practice, practice.*

*Baseball legend and humorist, Yogi Berra, famously said,
"Baseball is ninety percent mental. The other half is physical."

Directions:

Use the clues (problems) to find the numbers that will solve the puzzle. Write the numbers in words on the puzzle. (For instance, if the answer is $\frac{3}{5}$, write *threefifths*. Do not use a hyphen.) Reduce the answers to lowest terms unless directed otherwise.

Across

7. $\frac{1}{8} \div \frac{2}{5} =$

8. $6\frac{6}{7} \div \frac{6}{7} =$

9. $15 \div 1\frac{1}{2} =$

10. $2\frac{1}{2} \div \frac{5}{8} =$

11. $\frac{10}{27} \div \frac{5}{9} =$

13. $4\frac{1}{6} \div \frac{5}{12} =$

15. $2\frac{5}{11} \div \frac{9}{11} =$

17. $\frac{24}{91} \div \frac{4}{7} =$

19. $4\frac{1}{2} \div \frac{3}{4} =$

20. $\frac{1}{36} \div \frac{5}{9} =$

Down

1. $\frac{5}{10} \div 1 =$

2. $\frac{6}{18} \div \frac{1}{2} = \frac{?}{9}$

3. $\frac{9}{10} \div \frac{9}{10} =$

4. $6 \div \frac{2}{3} =$

5. $\frac{5}{18} \div \frac{5}{6} =$

6. $\frac{1}{10} \div \frac{2}{15} =$

7. $\frac{4}{70} \div \frac{1}{7} =$

12. $2\frac{4}{5} \div \frac{14}{5} =$

14. $16\frac{2}{3} \div \frac{5}{6} =$

15. $\frac{90}{2} \div \frac{9}{2} =$

16. $\frac{20}{11} \div \frac{10}{11} =$

18. $4\frac{4}{5} \div \frac{4}{5} =$

Puzzle 25

DINING AT HOME

The Toad family headed for the Creekside Café. When they heard about the dinner special, they went home. Why did they change their minds? Solve the puzzle to find out.

1 Color the puzzle.

- Look at each fraction in the puzzle.
- If the value is = or > $\frac{1}{2}$, color the section green.
- If the value is < $\frac{1}{2}$, color the section any color you choose.

KEY	
	k = $\frac{9}{13}$
b = $\frac{1}{8}$	l = $\frac{3}{5}$ or $\frac{3}{4}$
d = $\frac{4}{5}$	p = $\frac{6}{7}$
e = $\frac{9}{10}$	o = $\frac{11}{12}$
f = $\frac{5}{8}$	r = $\frac{2}{3}$
g = $\frac{1}{2}$	s = $\frac{5}{7}$
k = $\frac{2}{5}$	t = $\frac{1}{6}$
i = $\frac{7}{8}$	y = $\frac{5}{6}$

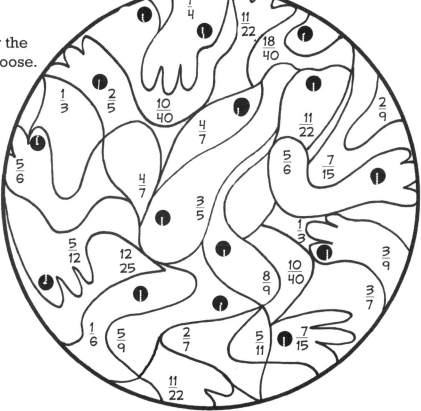

2 Find the answer.

On the Dinner sign, the numbers of the ten problems are written below the letters. Solve each problem. When you get the answer, find it on the KEY. Write the matching letter in the space (or spaces) with the problem number. *(For example, find the letter that matches the answer to problem # 1. Write that letter in the two spaces above the number 1.)*

DINNER SPECIAL
$15.00
All You Can Eat

—— —— —— —— —— —— ——
5   1   7   2   9   3   6

—— —— —— —— —— —— —— ——
4   1   10 5   9   3   5   8

1) $\frac{4}{3} \times \frac{1}{2} =$

2) $\frac{1}{15} \div \frac{1}{9} =$

3) $\frac{3}{10} \times 3 =$

4) $1\frac{1}{4} \times \frac{1}{2} =$

5) $\frac{2}{5} \times 1\frac{1}{4} =$

6) $\frac{2}{3} \div \frac{5}{6} =$

7) $\frac{7}{4} \times \frac{1}{2} =$

8) $2\frac{1}{7} \times \frac{1}{3} =$

9) $1\frac{1}{2} \times \frac{1}{2} =$

10) $\frac{11}{48} \div \frac{1}{4} =$

Name_____

THE MAGIC NUMBER HAT

Marvin the Magician can pull rabbits from a hat.
His hat has some magic of its own.

Directions:

Every row of numbers in the hat (horizontal or vertical)
has the same sum. This sum is the "magic number"
for this magic square. There are ten sums to find.
Fill in the missing numbers.

What is the magic number? _____

Prestidigitation!

(Oh, my stars! It worked!)

THE ELUSIVE PUNCH LINE

Why did the turkey cross the road? You'll have to break the code to find out.

Directions:

Solve the problems. Each numerical answer is the code number that matches a letter. Find the number on the Alphabet Key. Write the matching letter on the line above the problem number. This will reveal the punch line.

Alphabet Key

A = 396.2
C = 4.48
D = 27.74
E = 7.77
F = 52.71
G = 39.62
H = 39.41
I = 6.11
K = 1.86
L = 1.33
N = 64.479
O = 7.42
P = 31.5
R = 6.006
S = 20.7
T = 0.51
U = 0.0055
W = 66.8
Y = 0.5
Z = 2.002

1. $4.21 - 3.7 =$
2. $0.65 - 0.15 =$
3. $21.6 - 0.9 =$
4. $64.9 - 0.421 =$
5. $23.6 - 2.9 =$
6. $8.17 - 0.4 =$
7. $51.6 - 49.74 =$
8. $6.62 - 0.51 =$
9. $53.41 - 0.7 =$
10. $55.5 - 54.99 =$
11. $452.8 - 56.6 =$

12. $68.5 - 1.7 =$
13. $40.1 - 0.69 =$
14. $56.61 - 3.9 =$
15. $8.4 - 3.92 =$
16. $77.07 - 69.3 =$
17. $100.01 - 60.6 =$
18. $26.52 - 22.04 =$
19. $402 - 5.8 =$
20. $8.14 - 0.72 =$
21. $12.01 - 5.9 =$
22. $32.44 - 4.7 =$

GOBBLE,
GOBBLE!

HUNGRY FOR DECIMALS

Somebody's got a craving for cake. Multiply along as you follow this hungry decimal muncher.

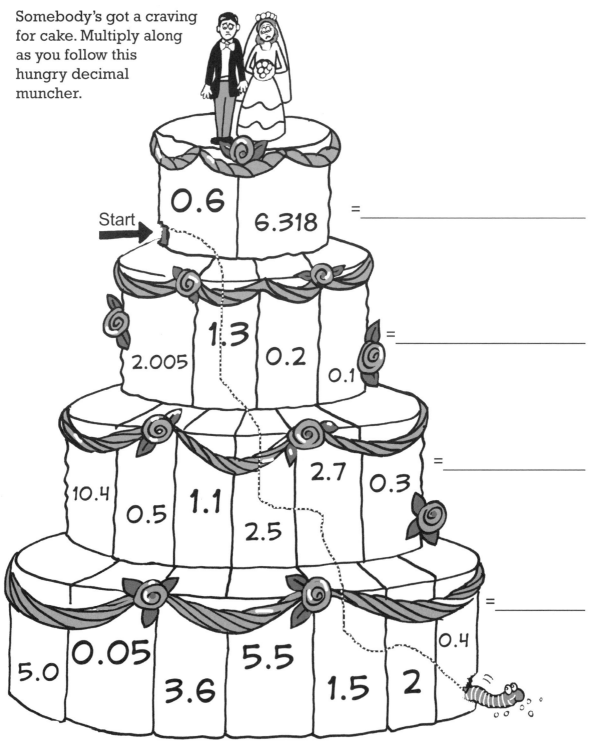

Start

0.6   6.318   = _____

1.3   0.2
2.005   0.1   = _____

10.4   1.1   2.7   0.3
0.5   2.5   = _____

5.0   0.05   5.5   0.4
3.6   1.5   2   = _____

Directions:

A. Find the product of each tier by multiplying the slices. Write each product.

B. Then follow the path of the hungry worm. Multiply the slices as he eats his way through them. The product of the worm's munching trip can be found on one slice of cake. Which slice is it?

Name_____

UNDERWATER SEARCH

A swishy swimmer slipped away from the City Aquarium. Can you find him in the pond?

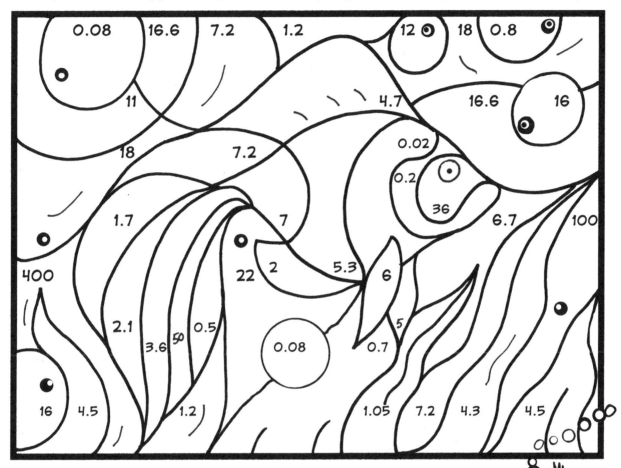

Directions:

Solve each group of problems. Find the answers in the puzzle and color in the answer spaces with that group's color. Complete all groups and describe what you find.

Green

1) $16.8 \div 16 =$

2) $107.1 \div 23.8 =$

3) $67.2 \div 56 =$

4) $94.6 \div 22 =$

5) $94.5 \div 21 =$

Yellow

6) $15.4 \div 2.2 =$

7) $64.8 \div 1.8 =$

8) $0.4 \div 20 =$

Blue

9) $93.6 \div 13 =$

10) $80.4 \div 12 =$

11) $11 \div 0.5 =$

12) $66.4 \div 4 =$

13) $1{,}000 \div 2.5 =$

14) $3{,}600 \div 500 =$

15) $330 \div 3.3 =$

16) $92.4 \div 8.4 =$

17) $156.24 \div 21.7 =$

18) $63.08 \div 3.8 =$

19) $165.6 \div 9.2 =$

20) $93.96 \div 78.3 =$

21) $4.41 \div 6.3 =$

22) $45 \div 2.5 =$

Pink

23) $42.4 \div 8 =$

24) $3 \div 0.5 =$

25) $3.32 \div 16.6 =$

26) $46.5 \div 9.3 =$

Orange

27) $15.3 \div 9 =$

28) $56.4 \div 12 =$

29) $1.55 \div 3.1 =$

30) $101 \div 50.5 =$

31) $64.8 \div 18 =$

JIGSAW DECIMALS

You won't find the answers until you put the puzzle back together.

Directions:

enigma

Copy the puzzle pieces (page 36) onto a piece of heavy paper.

Cut out the jigsaw pieces carefully.

Put the puzzle together.

Look for the following things on the puzzle.

MYSTERY

Find a number that is ...
(If the number is not there, write NO.)

1. the sum of 31.86 and 10.64

2. the product of 0.22 and 312.5

3. the difference between 8.45 and 7.55

4. the number that is closest to the square of 6.6

5. the missing divisor: $3.96 \div ? = 3.6$

6. the number that is thirty-five thousandths more than 42.465

7. the sum of $41.24 + 83.6 + 108.96 + 99.2$

8. the number that is twenty and two-hundredths less than 88.77

9. the number that is one-fourth of 1333.2

UNKNOWN

10. a number that is less than 0.0999

11. the missing quotient: $1.089 \div 0.99 =$

12. the product of 15.15 and 22

13. the difference between 89.06 and 87.96

14. the sum of 79.3 and 87.06 and 103.55 and 63.39

question

15. Write a new number onto the puzzle in the lower left-hand corner piece. This number should be the product of 11.01 and 0.11.

Use with the puzzle on page 37.

JIGSAW DECIMALS, CONTINUED

Use with page 36.

Name_____

CANAL CONUNDRUM

Marco heads off on his new houseboat to cruise the canal. Where is he going?

Directions:

Start with Marco's boat. When you come to an intersection, solve the problem in the arrow box. Take the route that contains the correct answer. You will not follow the letters in alphabetical order. Where does Marco end the trip?_____ Which intersection did he miss? _____

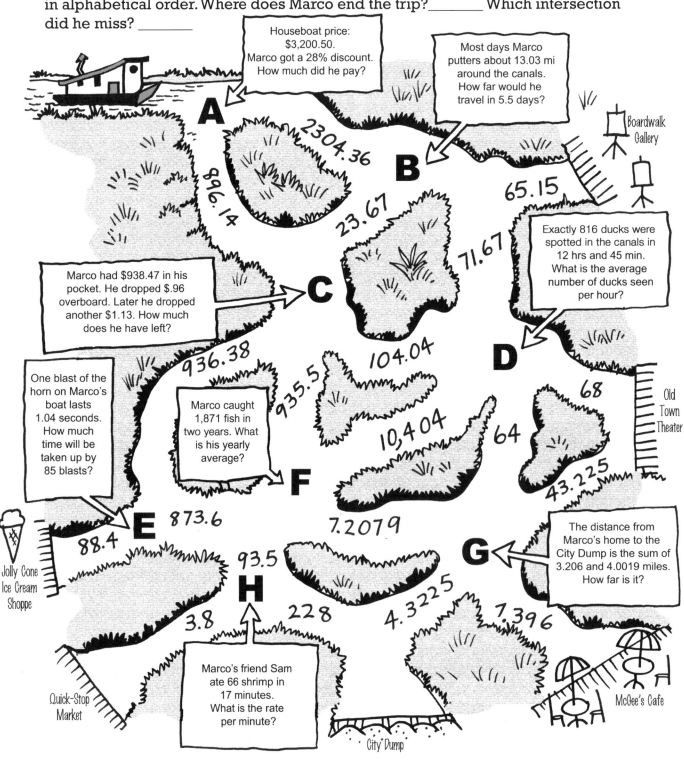

Houseboat price:
$3,200.50.
Marco got a 28% discount.
How much did he pay?

Most days Marco putters about 13.03 mi around the canals. How far would he travel in 5.5 days?

Marco had $938.47 in his pocket. He dropped $.96 overboard. Later he dropped another $1.13. How much does he have left?

Exactly 816 ducks were spotted in the canals in 12 hrs and 45 min. What is the average number of ducks seen per hour?

One blast of the horn on Marco's boat lasts 1.04 seconds. How much time will be taken up by 85 blasts?

Marco caught 1,871 fish in two years. What is his yearly average?

The distance from Marco's home to the City Dump is the sum of 3.206 and 4.0019 miles. How far is it?

Marco's friend Sam ate 66 shrimp in 17 minutes. What is the rate per minute?

Boardwalk Gallery

Old Town Theater

Jolly Cone Ice Cream Shoppe

Quick-Stop Market

City Dump

McGee's Cafe

A   2304.36   896.14

B   23.67   65.15   71.67

C   936.38   935.5   104.04

D   10,404   64   68   43.225

F   7.2079

E   873.6   88.4

H   93.5   228   3.8

G   4.3225   7.396

THE COVER-UP PUZZLE

It will take a cover-up to solve these puzzles.

Directions:

Each blank disc needs to be covered up with one of the loose discs. Pay close attention to the symbols between the circles as you try to solve the two puzzles.

Write the missing numbers. Then solve the three vertical problems in B.

A

$$6 \times -1 + \boxed{} = 1$$
$$\times \qquad + \qquad \times$$
$$\boxed{} \times \boxed{} - \boxed{} = 29$$
$$\div \qquad + \qquad +$$
$$\boxed{} \times \boxed{} \div \boxed{} = -4$$
$$= \qquad = \qquad =$$
$$-3 \qquad -6 \qquad -83$$

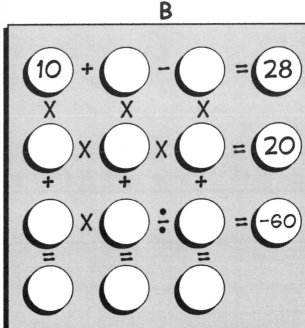

B

$$10 + \boxed{} - \boxed{} = 28$$
$$\times \qquad \times \qquad \times$$
$$\boxed{} \times \boxed{} \times \boxed{} = 20$$
$$+ \qquad + \qquad +$$
$$\boxed{} \times \boxed{} \div \boxed{} = -60$$
$$= \qquad = \qquad =$$
$$\boxed{} \qquad \boxed{} \qquad \boxed{}$$

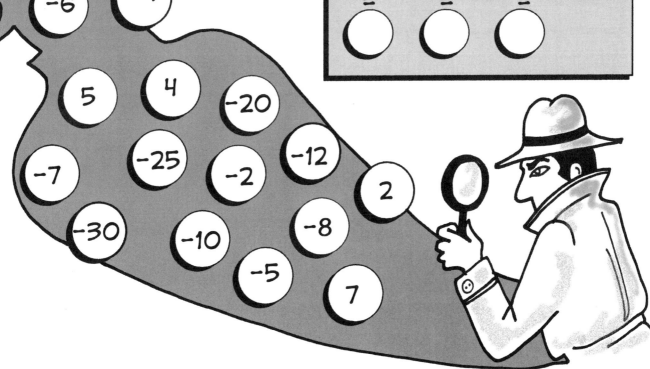

-6   -9   5   4   -20   -7   -25   -2   -12   -30   -10   -8   2   -5   7

Name_____

A PUZZLE WITH PRIDE

What prideful creature is hiding here? Let the colors bring him out of hiding.

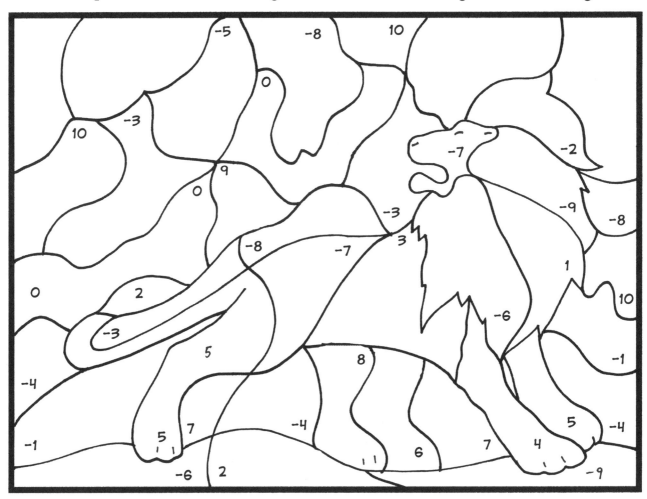

Directions:

Solve each problem. Find the answer in the puzzle. Fill the answer's space(s) with the color at the top of that group of problems.

shh!   click

Blue

1) 3 + (–8) =

2) –9 – (–6) =

3) 12 + (–12) =

4) –5 + 14 =

5) –6 + (–2) =

6) 5 – (–5) =

Green

7) 5 + 6 – 12 =

8) –3 + 9 =

9) –2 – 2 =

10) –13 + 20 =

Brown

11) 10 – 5 – 11 =

12) –7 – (–9) =

13) –22 + 13 =

Yellow

14) 0 – 7 =

15) –15 + 5 + 15 =

16) 6 + (–16) + 13 =

17) –7 + 11 =

Orange

18) –1 + 2 =

19) 18 + (–20) =

20) –5 – (–13) =

Name_____

A Strange Bird

Do the math and follow the dots to reveal the creature
that's got all the other birds chattering in amazement.

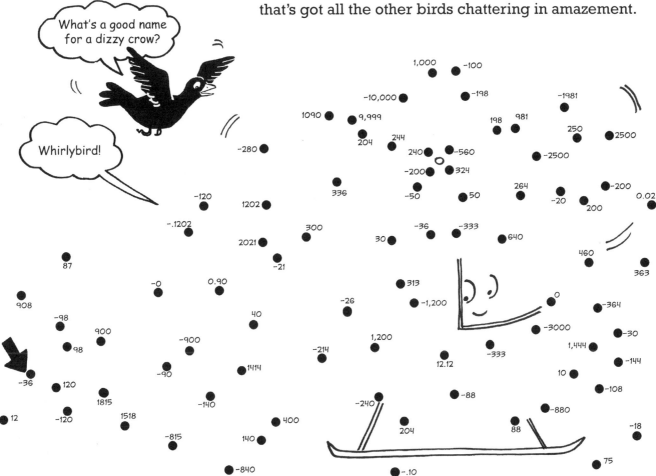

Directions:

Solve the first problem. Draw a line from the ARROW to the first answer.
Continue connecting the answer dots in order as you solve the problems.

1. $-7 \times 14 =$
2. $-30 \times (-30) =$
3. $-4 \times (-10) =$
4. $13 \times 2 \times (-1) =$
5. $5(-3 + 9) =$
6. $-9 \times 4 =$
7. $25 \times (-8) =$
8. $-601 \times (-2) =$
9. $-7 \times (-4) \times (-10) =$
10. $(-8 \times 6) \times (-5) =$
11. $1000 \times (-10) =$

12. $-6 \times 33 =$
13. $-40 \times 14 =$
14. $-25 \times 2 \times (-5) =$
15. $-50 \times (-50) =$
16. $100 \times (-2) =$
17. $-18 \times (-18) =$
18. $3 \times (-111) =$
19. $8 \times 80 =$
20. $-2 \times 0 \times (-6) =$
21. $91 \times (-4) =$
22. $10(5 - 8) =$

23. $12 \times (-12) =$
24. $-27 \times 4 =$
25. $-20 \times (-2) \times (-22) =$
26. $44 \times 2 \times 1 =$
27. $-4 \times -51 =$
28. $20 \times (-3 \times 4) =$
29. $5 \times 7 \times (-4) =$
30. $-121 \times (-15) =$
31. $-6 \times (-4) \times (-5) =$
32. $(4 + 5) \times (-4) =$

Name_____

INTEGER CRISS-CROSS

The integers on each pattern strip of the blanket have a unique relationship.
Figure out what it is and finish the puzzles by supplying the missing numbers.

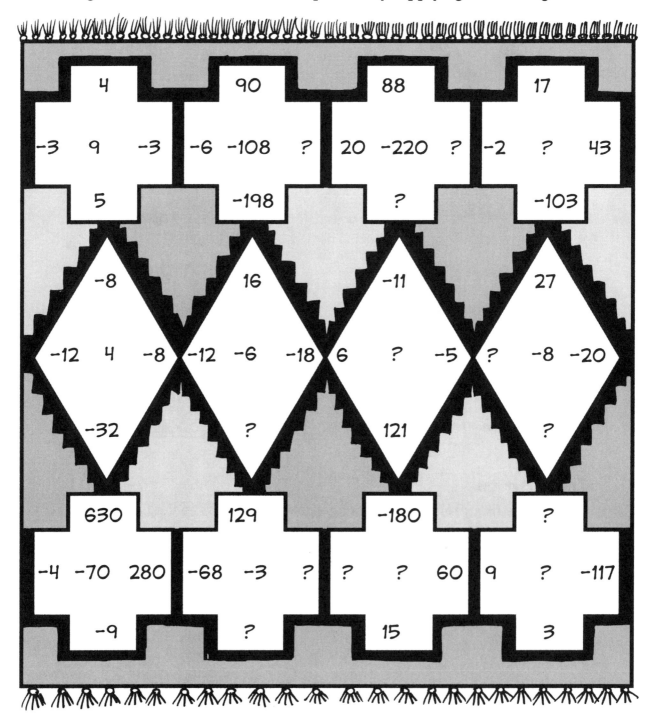

Directions:

To solve each row, carefully examine the numbers in the first cross (or diamond) to find
the relationship between them. Write the relationship as a rule. Then follow the rule to
fill in the missing numbers on the other three shapes in that row.

Name_____

ESCAPE FROM THE SWAMP

Avoid wrong answers and other hazards as you find your way out of the swamp.

Directions:

You're lost in the middle of a deep swamp. Choose a path and start checking the problem solutions. When you come to a WRONG answer, choose a different path. Follow the path of CORRECT solutions to the ESCAPE sign.

ALPHABET SOUP

This puzzle will lead you to things you never want to find in your soup!

Directions:

An exponential number is written on each letter in the puzzle.
Match each value below (problems 1–18) to the correct number
in the puzzle. Color the letter that holds the number. (Two
problems have two correct answers!) Then, use the colored
letters to make words. Each word must name something you do
NOT want to find in your soup. Write five or more words that can
be made from the colored letters.

1. 1,000,000	7. 1	13. 324
2. 512	8. 225	14. 32
3. 8	9. 729	15. 25,600
4. 160,000	10. 8,000,000	16. 1089
5. 125	11. 64	17. 289
6. 343	12. 243	18. 625

Name_____

Roots + Radicals Race

Once you know the values of these roots and radicals, you can get all the mice to the finish line.

Directions:

Four mice race for goodies from the top to the bottom of the puzzle. Notice where each mouse begins and ends the race. Find a path for each mouse. The path can go to any adjoining item (horizontally, vertically, or diagonally) but can go only to an item of decreasing value. **Each mouse must pass through snacks in at least three different columns.**

Name_____

EXPONENT MATCH-UP

Every piece of Pattern A (left) has a partner in Pattern B (right). Get busy matching them up—but watch out for the missing numbers.

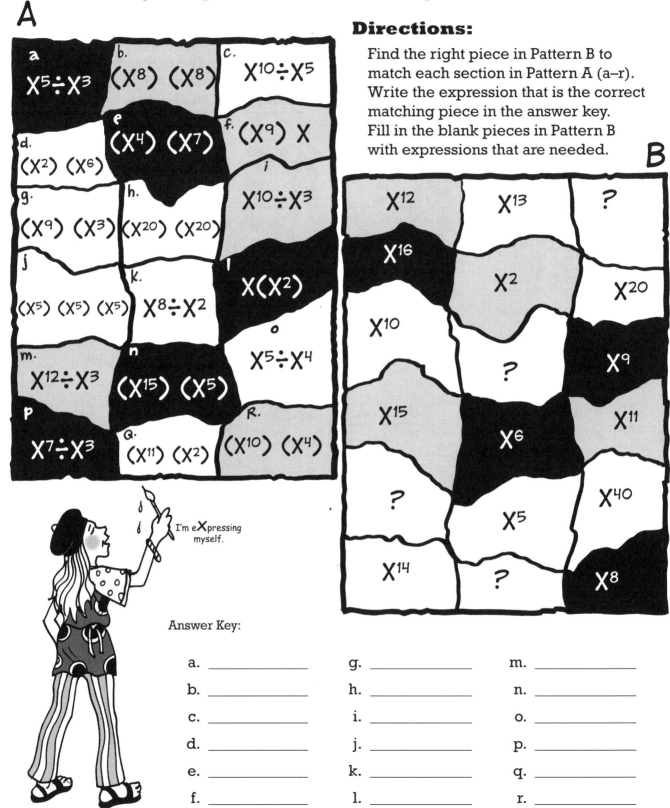

Directions:

Find the right piece in Pattern B to match each section in Pattern A (a–r). Write the expression that is the correct matching piece in the answer key. Fill in the blank pieces in Pattern B with expressions that are needed.

A

a. $X^5 \div X^3$
b. $(X^8)(X^8)$
c. $X^{10} \div X^5$
d. $(X^2)(X^6)$
e. $(X^4)(X^7)$
f. $(X^9)X$
g. $(X^9)(X^3)$
h. $(X^{20})(X^{20})$
i. $X^{10} \div X^3$
j. $(X^5)(X^5)(X^5)$
k. $X^8 \div X^2$
l. $X(X^2)$
m. $X^{12} \div X^3$
n. $(X^{15})(X^5)$
o. $X^5 \div X^4$
p. $X^7 \div X^3$
q. $(X^{11})(X^2)$
r. $(X^{10})(X^4)$

B

X^{12} X^{13} ?
X^{16} X^2 X^{20}
X^{10} ? X^9
X^{15} X^6 X^{11}
? X^5 X^{40}
X^{14} ? X^8

I'm e**X**pressing myself.

Answer Key:

a. _____   g. _____   m. _____

b. _____   h. _____   n. _____

c. _____   i. _____   o. _____

d. _____   j. _____   p. _____

e. _____   k. _____   q. _____

f. _____   l. _____   r. _____

Name_____

Puzzle It! Math Computation Puzzles　　46

HIDDEN PROVERB

Crack the code to reveal this wise and witty Burmese proverb.

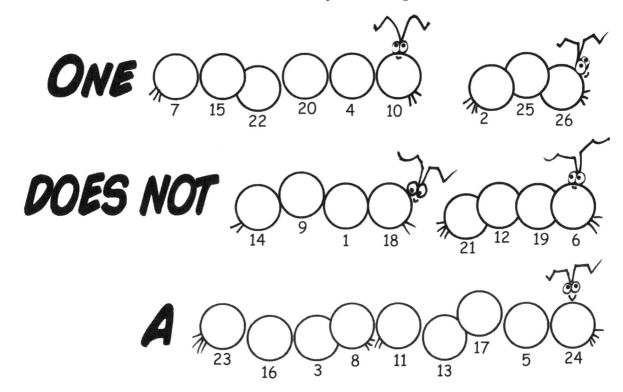

ALPHABET KEY

A = y^{10}	I = 200	P = 125
B = 4	J = 50	R = 30
C = 37	K = x^6	S = x^9
D = y^2	L = 45	T = y^7
E = 25	M = x^5	U = x^{100}
F = 0	N = 10	W = x^{20}
G = 1,280	O = 53	Y = x^{14}

Directions:

Solve the problems. Each answer matches a letter in the Alphabet Key. Write that letter in the space above the problem number. If you solve the problems correctly, the puzzle will reveal the proverb.

1. $81 - 28 =$

2. $10^3 - 30^2 - 55 =$

3. $13^2 - 159 =$

4. $10^2 \div 4 =$

5. $y^2 + 0 =$

6. $3^3 - 17 =$

7. $11^2 - 10^2 - 17 =$

8. $(y^5)(y^2) =$

9. $6^3 - 171 =$

10. $9^2 - 7^2 - 22 =$

11. $2^8 - 56 =$

12. $14^2 - 143 =$

13. $5^5 - 3,000 =$

14. $(x^7)(x^2) =$

15. $17^2 - 259 =$

16. $16 + 3^2 =$

17. $2^6 - 39 =$

18. $x^{25} \div x^5 =$

19. $(x^{10})(x^{10}) =$

20. $x^9 \div x^3 =$

21. $y^6 \div y^4 =$

22. $9^3 - 676 =$

23. $5^2 + 12 =$

24. $2^4 + 9 =$

25. $11^2 - 96 =$

26. $80 \times 2^4 =$

Name_____

DON'T START THE GAME

Don't start the BINGO game until you have polished up your equation-solving skills.

B	I	N	G	O
0.01	9	82	101	15
13	-9	33	6	60
0.15	-2	-15	16	0.1
-6	11	2.2	1.5	-8
22	10	8	2	-11

Directions:

Get some coins, buttons, or stones to use as Bingo markers.

Solve all the equations. (Some problems have two correct answers.) Find each solution on the Bingo board. Cover that number with a marker. Some squares might get more than one marker!

Which Bingo squares got more than one marker?
_____
On which problem were you able to call **Bingo**?
_____

1. $75 - x = -7$
2. $x^2 + 12 = 133$
3. $b - 1.6 = -1.5$
4. $18n = 108$
5. $24.2 \div d = 11$
6. $73 - x^2 = -8$
7. $3y = 4.5$
8. $p - 20 = -7$
9. $q + 30 = 22$
10. $n - (-15) = 0$
11. $x^2 = 3600$
12. $y \div 3 = 11$
13. $x^5 = -32$
14. $6.5 + x = 6.65$

15. $-15y \div 5 = 33$
16. $-40 \div n = -20$
17. $4w = 8.8$
18. $3a^2 = 300$
19. $9 - b = 8.99$
20. $a - 100 = 1$
21. $40n = 880$
22. $k + 6 = 0$
23. $7y = 112$
24. $d^2 - d = 56$
25. $14b = -112$
26. $3x + 34 = 79$
27. $50 - 4x = 26$
28. $3x = -27$

Name_____

COOL CALCULATIONS

Solve the equations quickly, before the ice cream melts!

Directions:

Find the value of x in each equation. Write the solution in the correct squares on the puzzle.

Across

3. $1000 - x = 101$

6. $x \div 6 = 11$

7. $x + 193 = 500$

9. $3x + 5 = 155$

10. $x \div 2 = 22$

12. $50 + x - 11 = 150$

14. $2x^2 = 288$

15. $3x = 99$

Down

1. $-x + 59 = 40$

2. $-5 + x = -5$

3. $x - 48 = 38$

4. $4x = 372$

5. $1000 - 2x = 450$

6. $\sqrt{x} = 8$

8. $x \div 3 = 47$

11. $x^2 = 441$

13. $x \div 5 = 3$

Name_____

GOOD ADVICE

Solve the equations, break the code, and get some good advice—all at the same time!

Directions:

A. The solution to each equation will match a letter in the alphabet. Choose the letter of the alphabet that has that numerical position in the alphabet. (i.e., 1 = A; 26 = Z). Write down each letter as you solve the equation.

B. When you have found all the letters, unscramble the missing words.

SOME GOOD ADVICE: There are two things you should never hold at the same time:

a __ __ __ and a __ __ __ __ __ __ __ __ __ __ __ __

FIRST WORD CLUES

1. $x^8 + 45 = 46$

2. $100 - x^4 = 19$

3. $80 = x + 60$

I should have listened!

SECOND WORD CLUES

4. $x - 28 + 12 + 3 = 8$

5. $5x^2 = 125$

6. $224 - 55n = 57n$

7. $-75\,b = -1500$

8. $35a = 665$

9. $p - (-80) = 100$

10. $-2y \div -3 = 12$

11. $95d - 10(d + 5) = 290$

12. $12 - 2g = -26$

13. $2n^2 = 882$

A COLORFUL CHARACTER

Solve the equations to get the colors right on this awesome creature.

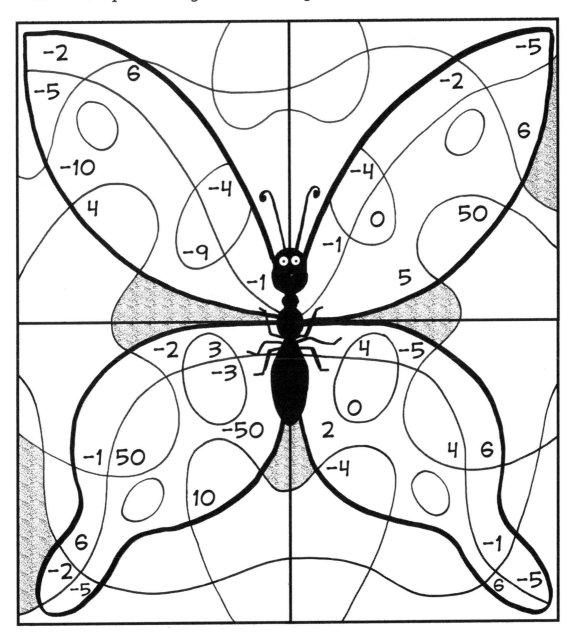

Directions:

Each group of equations has a color label. As you solve each equation, color all the spaces in the puzzle that show the answer.

Dark Brown	**Yellow**	**Blue**	**Red**	**Orange**
1. $-12 + x = -14$	5. $5c = -50$	9. $4000 \div g = 400$	11. $x - 7 = -7$	14. $-17 - c = -20$
2. $5y = 30$	6. $d - 12 = -7$		12. $15y = -45$	15. $40n = 2000$
3. $3b + 15 = 0$	7. $60n = 120$	10. $-2n = 8$	13. $b + 4 = -5$	16. $40a = 160$
4. $12 + x = 11$	8. $x + 70 = 20$			

Name_____

DOMINO EQUATIONS

Practice equation solutions using the spots on these dominoes!

Directions:

Assume that the number of spots on each domino is represented by **(x, y)** where **x** = the number of spots on one end, and **y** = the number of spots on the other end.

Decide which domino in the puzzle fits with each equation. Write the letter of the domino that matches each one.

_____ 1. $x^2 - y = 12$

_____ 2. $y + x = 2$

_____ 3. $2(x + y) = 12$

_____ 4. $x^2 + 2x = 35$

_____ 5. $-y - x = -12$

_____ 6. $6x + y = 14$

_____ 7. $x + 3y = 18$

_____ 8. $10(x + 2y) = 80$

_____ 9. $x + x + y = 13$

_____ 10. $x - 2y = 1$

_____ 11. $xy = 6$

_____ 12. $xy + x = 5$

_____ 13. $x - y = -4$

_____ 14. $x + x + y = 15$

_____ 15. $5(x + y) = 55$

CLOCKWISE VARIABLES

Many chords originate from the center of a circle, . . . so many solutions can result from an equation with two variables.

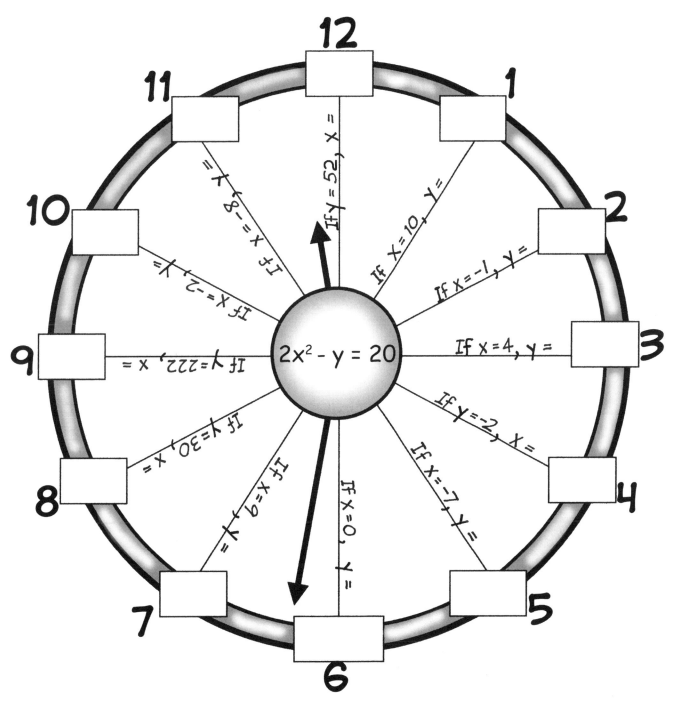

Directions:

When an equation has more than one variable, it can have more than one solution. There is just one equation here. It is in the center of the clock. Take time to find the missing variable for each number on the clock.

KERNEL COMPUTATIONS

WHAT DO YOU GET WHEN YOU CROSS AN EAR OF CORN WITH A SPICY PEPPER?

Directions:

Solve the first problem. Draw a line from the START dot to the first answer. Continue connecting the answer dots in order as you solve the 25 problems. If an answer has a letter beside it, write that letter in the kernel(s) with that answer. The letters will spell the answer to the riddle (above).

1. $\frac{15}{10} \times \frac{1}{3} =$

2. $48 - 50 =$

3. $27,000 \div 90 =$

4. $13.5 - 14 =$

5. $-144 \div (-6) =$

6. $6^2 - 16 =$

7. $11^2 =$

8. $25 \times 16 =$

9. $30 - 29.95 =$

10. $2.2 \times 4.6 =$

11. $10^2 =$

12. $50 \times 400 =$

13. $-5000 \div 500 =$

14. $2 \times 33 + 11 =$

15. $100 - 78 - 13 =$

16. $\frac{2}{15} \div \frac{1}{5} =$

17. $60.5 \div 11 =$

18. $-45 - (-40) =$

19. $9^2 =$

20. $-4 \times (-50) =$

21. $4000 \div 50 =$

22. $\frac{16}{20} - \frac{2}{10} =$

23. $100 - 34 =$

24. $3.75 \div 7.5 =$

25. $13 - (-12) =$

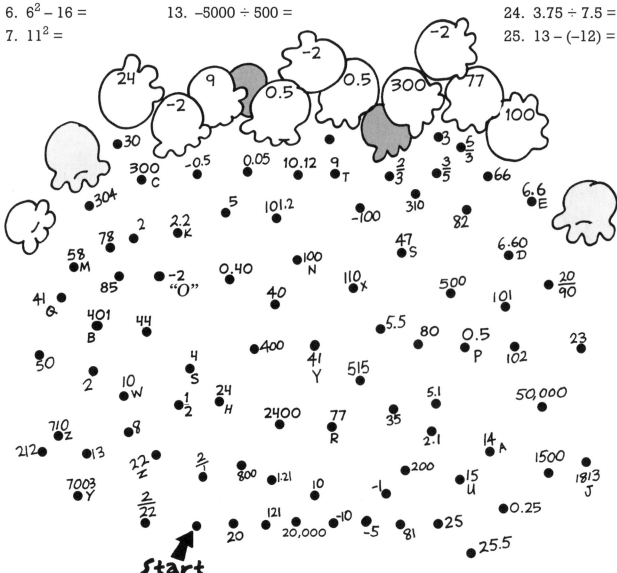

Start

Name_____

WHO GETS THE PIZZA?

Puzzle 48

The pizza delivery girl has forgotten which customer gets the tenth pizza.

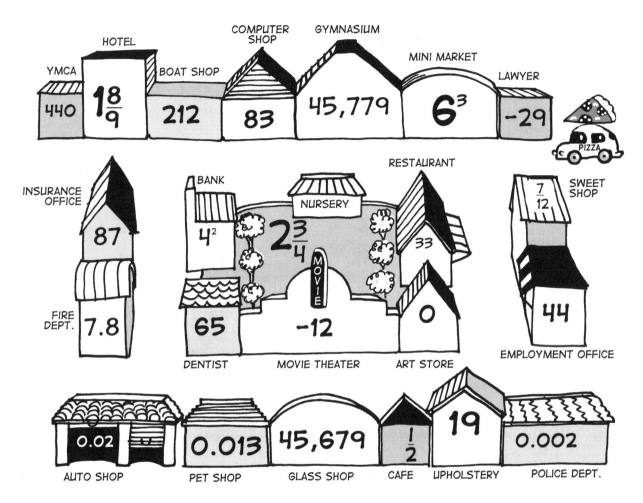

Directions:

Solve each problem. Find the location on the map with that answer.
Write the first letter of the business on the line next to the problem.
When all nine problems are solved, unscramble the letters to find
the name of the place for the last delivery.

		letter			*letter*
1.	$-15 - (-9) + 6 - 12 =$	_____	5.	$\frac{7}{16} \div \frac{3}{4} =$	_____
2.	$2958 \div 34 =$	_____	6.	$x = 216$	_____
3.	$0.022 \times 20{,}000 =$	_____	7.	$55{,}555 - 9876 =$	_____
4.	$8.011 - 7.991 =$	_____	8.	$\frac{1}{2} \times 5\frac{1}{2} =$	_____
			9.	$6(-3 + 1) + 31 =$	_____

10. Letters to unjumble:

The last delivery goes to: _____

Name _____

She's Got Clues!

When Detective Kay Lever got to the scene of the crime, she found three clues. Follow the clues to identify the suspect.

THE MYSTERY:

Granny Cooper came home to her apartment to find the kitchen torn apart. Her special seven-layer cake was gone, cupboards were open, dishes were knocked off the sink, chairs were upset. In the living room, pillows were knocked off the couch, lamps were turned over, most of the furniture was smeared with a sticky substance, and the floor was strewn with papers and crumbs. She called the police.

THE CLUES:

Three clues were left on the counter top:

#1. A set of unsolved math problems.

#2. An Alphabet Code Key

#3. A piece of paper with some blanks.

When clues 1, 2, and 3 are put together, they will point to the likely suspect.

Directions:

Figure out what the clues reveal. When you end up with some letters, unscramble them to find that last clue, telling the fourth thing left on the countertop. Make a guess as to whom the culprit might be.

CLUE #1

1. $(80 \div 16) \times 200 =$

2. $\sqrt{160,000} \times 8 + 10 =$

3. $(-25 \div 5) + 30 =$

4. $(\frac{1}{2} \times \frac{3}{4}) \div (\frac{1}{3}) =$

5. $(0.52 \times 0.3) + 7.4 - 1.01 =$

6. $225,400 \div 70 =$

7. $1.5 + \frac{3}{4} + 16\frac{3}{4} + 6 =$

8. $19.53 - 12.93 =$

9. $-77 - (-70) =$

CLUE #2

A = 6.6	F = 6.07	P = 25
C = −25	I = 3210	R = 3220
D = 3620	N = 1000	S = 6.546
E = $1\frac{3}{4}$	O = −9	T = $1\frac{1}{8}$
		W = −7

CLUE #3

CALCULATIONS ON TARGET

Calculate correctly to complete the target. Then use it for a good math game.

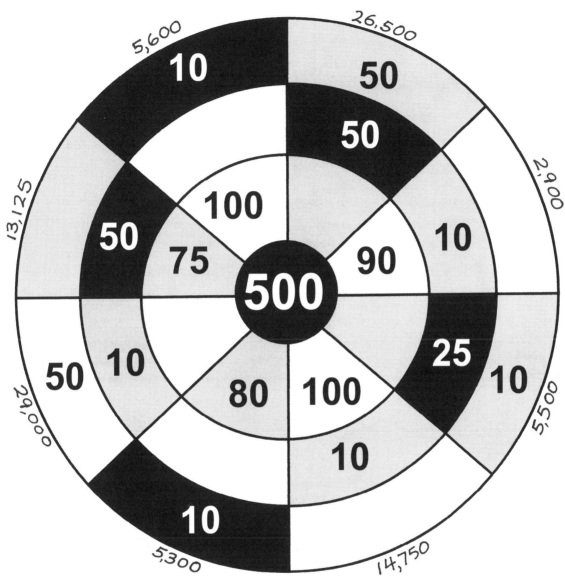

Directions:

1. Find the missing numbers for the target. For each slice, begin with the number in the center. Move out from the center. Add the first number (in the first ring), subtract the second, and multiply by the third. The answers are shown for each "slice" outside the largest ring.

2. When you have found the missing numbers, get some coins and a friend to play this game.
   Lay the target on a table. Flick a coin across the target and watch where it lands. Flick a second coin. Find the product of the two numbers. The second player does the same. The object of the game is to try to get a larger sum than your opponent. Play the game again. This time, find the difference between the two numbers. Try to get the smallest answer.

Name_____

ANSWER KEY

Puzzle 1 (pg 6)
A Case Of Missing Addends

Puzzle 2 (pg 7)
A Card Puzzler
Missing cards:
- A-1: 10 of clubs
- A-3: 6 of clubs
- A-4: 7 of hearts
- B-1: 5 of hearts
- B-2: 4 of hearts
- B-3: 8 of hearts
- C-2: 9 of hearts
- D-2: 2 of clubs

Puzzle 3 (pg 8)
Caught in the Web

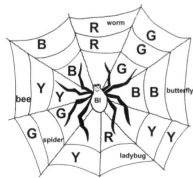

Puzzle 4 (pg 9)
Straight from the Honeycomb

Puzzle 5 (pg 10)
Something's Dancing

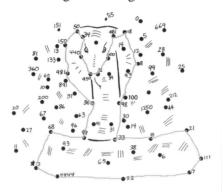

Puzzle 6 (pg 11)
Mystery Hoops
In all "wedges," the number in the center is the difference between the other two numbers.

A. The two outer numbers have reversed digits.
   Done: 98 – 89 = 9
   Moving clockwise
   Missing number: 14
   Missing number: 73
   Missing number: 18
   Missing number: 72
   Missing number: 15

B. The two outer numbers are related in this way: In one, each digit is 2 greater than the same digit in the other number.
   Done: 34 – 12 = 22
   Moving clockwise:
   Missing number: 62
   Missing number: 36
   Missing number: 22
   Missing number: 52
   Missing number: 22

C. One of the outer numbers is formed by taking the hundreds digit of the other number and moving it to the ones place.
   Done: 712 – 127 = 585
   Moving clockwise:
   Missing number: 876
   Missing number: 209
   Missing number: 162
   Missing number: 303
   Missing number: 553

Puzzle 7 (pg 12)
Take Note

1. 30
2. 26
3. 75
4. 273
5. 48
6. 2,209
7. 1,001
8. 591
9. 417
10. 172

The tune is the beginning to "Row, Row, Row Your Boat"

Puzzle 8 (pg 13)
The Amazing 4
The path to the door follows these problems (answers containing 4):

$$52 \times 7 = 364$$
$$32 \times 45 = 1440$$
$$97 \times 52 = 5044$$
$$22 \times 641 = 14,102$$
$$540 \times 10 = 5,400$$
$$81 \times 5 = 405$$
$$846 \times 50 = 42,300$$
$$179 \times 6 = 1074$$
$$150 \times 36 = 5400$$
$$45 \times 94 = 4230$$

Puzzle 9 (pg 14)
Frantic Antics

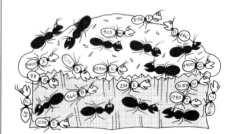

These ants should be colored red:
1. 78 (C)

2. 540 (O)
3. 4050 (A)
4. 1111 (T)
5. 576 (U)
6. 1040 (A)
7. 2304 (N)
8. 8256 (C)
9. 23,188 (N)
10. 10,080 (T)

The answer to the riddle is: accountant

Puzzle 10 (pg 15)
Treasure Map Numbers

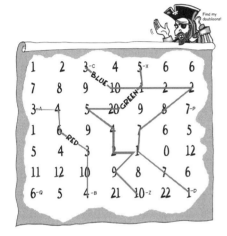

Red line, A to Z =
   3 x 4 x 6 x 3 x 10 x 4 = 8,640

Black line, C to D =
   3 x 10 x 1 x 2 x 2 x 8 x 7 x 1 x 7
   x 1 = 47,040

Blue line, P to Q =
   any series of adjoining numbers
   that includes the zero

Green line, X to Z =
   5 x 1 x 20 x 5 x 4 x 2 x 1 x 9 x 10
   = 72,000

Puzzle 11 (pg 16)
Never, Ever Smile At One
Figure is a crocodile.

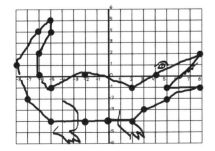

Puzzle 12 (pg 17)
After-Dinner Math

Mathematician is saying:
"This bill doesn't add up."

1. 40	30. 74
2. 14	31. 43
3. 41	32. 25
4. 3	33. 85
5. 21	34. 9
6. 63	35. 58
7. 38	36. 19
8. 42	37. 69
9. 54	38. 59
10. 6	39. 81
11. 49	40. 34
12. 29	41. 89
13. 47	42. 95
14. 56	43. 71
15. 2	44. 90
16. 36	45. 31
17. 16	46. 51
18. 45	47. 98
19. 76	48. 86
20. 23	49. 10
21. 65	50. 20
22. 83	51. 7
23. 5	52. 11
24. 27	53. 87
25. 78	54. 60
26. 1	55. 96
27. 67	56. 91
28. 18	57. 94
29. 61	

Puzzle 13 (pg 18)
Bite Into Bingo

1. 8, R4   (O–cookie)
2. 9, R24   (N–banana)
3. 8, R14   (B–popcorn)
4. 14, R11   (I–milkshake)
5. 8, R13   (O–pizza)
6. 7, R16   (G–apple)
7. 6, R2   (I–hot dog)
8. 45, R12   (N–cupcake)
9. 10, R10   (B–pizza)
10. 15, R20   (N–taco)
11. 12, R5   (G–pineapple)
12. 7, R1   (G–ice cream cone)

Puzzle 14 (pg 19)
Dial Up A Puzzle

1. 1, R 12
2. 4, R 6
3. 2, R 16
4. 2, R 17
5. 1, R 37
6. 5, R 2

Puzzle 15 (pg 20)
A Strange Law

1. 45 (G)
2. 63 (R)
3. 185 (H)
4. 99 (E)
5. 30 (I)
6. 9 (O)
7. 71 (S)
8. 98 (U)
9. 79 (P)
10. 99 (E)
11. 63 (R)
12. 63 (R)
13. 3 (B)
14. 30 (I)
15. 56 (N)
16. 56 (N)
17. 45 (G)
18. 56 (N)
19. 98 (U)
20. 41 (C)
21. 31 (Z)
22. 56 (N)
23. 41 (C)
24. 185 (H)
25. 30 (I)

The completed puzzle reads:
In Omaha, an old law prohibits
burping or sneezing in church.

Puzzle 16 (pg 21)
Domino Addition

1. 16

2. Circle domino with 6 dots
   and 6 dots.

3. The row near the top right
   (1 x 4 x 4 x 5 x 5 x 3 = 1200)

4. 4 + 0 + 0 + 5 + 5 + 5 = 19
   OR
   3 + 6 + 6 + 6 + 6 + 0 = 27

5. Vertical row on right
   (3 x 1 x 1 x 6 x 6 = 108)

Puzzle 17 (pg 22)
Number Jumble
1. 996
2. 2,627
3. 1,100
4. can't do this (1048)
5. 26,667
6. can't do this (9,753)
7. can't do this (995)
8. 9,990
9. 333
10. 103

Missing numbers needed: one of each: 4, 5, 8

Puzzle 18 (pg 23)
A Puzzling Painting

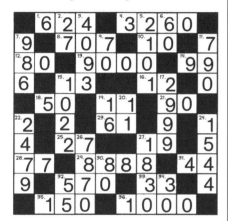

Across
1. 624
4. 3260
8. 707
10. 10
12. 80
13. 9000
14. 99
15. 13
16. 12
18. 50
19. 11
21. 90
23. 61
25. 27
27. 19
28. 77
29. 8888
31. 44
32. 570
33. 33
35. 150
36. 1000

Down
2. 27
3. 4093
5. 2101
6. 60
7. 986
9. 70
11. 790
15. 1022
17. 2999
19. 16
20. 11
22. 2479
24. 1544
26. 7870
27. 1830
30. 80
32. 55
34. 30

Puzzle 19 (pgs 24–25)
Bug Boggle

	A	B	C	D	E	F	G	H
1	L	A	D	Y	L	N	D	R
2	J	U	B	E	F	L	O	A
3	U	G	E	N	R	N	G	S
4	A	N	S	T	A	E	T	P
5	W	A	V	P	L	E	D	I

A–1	303 = L	E–1	303 = L
A–2	100 = J	E–2	18 = F
A–3	106 = U	E–3	29 = R
A–4	40 = A	E–4	40 = A
A–5	666 = W	E–5	303 = L
B–1	40 = A	F–1	50 = N
B–2	106 = U	F–2	303 = L
B–3	56 = G	F–3	50 = N
B–4	50 = N	F–4	900 = E
B–5	40 = A	F–5	900 = E
C–1	12 = D	G–1	12 = D
C–2	80 = B	G–2	85 = O
C–3	900 = E	G–3	56 = G
C–4	28 = S	G–4	313 = T
C–5	17 = V	G–5	12 = D
D–1	25 = Y	H–1	29 = R
D–2	900 = E	H–2	40 = A
D–3	50 = N	H–3	28 = S
D–4	313 = T	H–4	66 = P
D–5	66 = P	H–5	1000 = I

Some bug names that can be found are: bee, ant, fly, dragonfly, ladybug, beetle, wasp, gnat, spider, junebug

Puzzle 20 (pg 26)
A Star-Crossed Puzzle

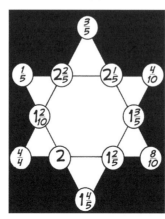

The magic number is $5\frac{1}{5}$.

Puzzle 21 (pg 27)
Sidewalk Challenge

a–b. $\frac{2}{5} + \frac{1}{7} = \frac{19}{35}$

c. $\frac{19}{35} + \frac{4}{10} = \frac{33}{35}$

d. $\frac{33}{35} - \frac{5}{35} = \frac{28}{35}$ or $\frac{4}{7}$

e. $\frac{4}{7} + \frac{2}{4} = 1\frac{1}{14}$

f. $1\frac{1}{14} + \frac{6}{14} = 1\frac{1}{2}$

g. $1\frac{1}{2} + 6\frac{1}{3} = 7\frac{5}{6}$

h. $7\frac{5}{6} - 3\frac{5}{12} = 4\frac{5}{12}$

i. $4\frac{5}{12} + \frac{5}{6} = 5\frac{1}{4}$

j. $5\frac{1}{4} + \frac{3}{10} = 5\frac{11}{20}$

k. $5\frac{11}{20} - 3\frac{1}{20} = 2\frac{1}{2}$

l. $2\frac{1}{2} - \frac{2}{3} = 1\frac{5}{6}$

m. $1\frac{5}{6} + 3\frac{1}{6} = 5$

n. $5 + \frac{3}{4} = 5\frac{3}{4}$

o. $5\frac{3}{4} + \frac{4}{5} = 6\frac{1}{4}$

p. $6\frac{1}{4} + \frac{1}{3} = 6\frac{7}{12}$

q. $6\frac{7}{12} + 2\frac{3}{4} = 9\frac{1}{3}$

r. Missing number is $-\frac{2}{3}$

Puzzle 22 (pg 28)
The Spin Cycle

1. $\frac{3}{8}$
2. $2\frac{1}{4}$
3. $\frac{8}{9}$
4. $5\frac{1}{6}$
5. $\frac{1}{2}$
6. $\frac{1}{8}$
7. $\frac{2}{3}$
8. $\frac{11}{100}$
9. $\frac{3}{4}$
10. $\frac{22}{49} - \frac{2}{7}$
11. $\frac{1}{9} + \frac{5}{6}$
12. $\frac{1}{5} + \frac{4}{5} + \frac{9}{11}$

Puzzle 23 (pg 29)
Missing Links

A. $\frac{7}{8}$
B. 1
C. $\frac{3}{5}$
D. $2\frac{1}{3}$
E. $\frac{1}{2}$
F. $\frac{2}{5}$
G. 1
H. $2\frac{4}{15}$

Puzzle with 8 links:
$\frac{2}{5} - \frac{1}{2} - \frac{3}{5} - \frac{7}{8} - 1 - 1 - 2\frac{4}{15} - 2\frac{1}{3}$

Puzzle 24 (pg 30)
Put It Into Words

Across	Down
7) five sixteenths	1) five tenths
8) eight	2) six ninths
9) ten	3) one
10) four	4) nine
11) two thirds	5) one third
13) ten	6) three fourths
15) three	7) four tenths
17) six thirteenths	12) one
19) six	14) twenty
20) one twentieth	15) ten
	16) two
	18) six

Puzzle 25 (pg 31)
Dining At Home

Part 1: Sections to be colored green: Fractions equal to or greater than $\frac{1}{2}$ are $\frac{4}{7}$; $\frac{5}{6}$; $\frac{3}{5}$; $\frac{8}{9}$; $\frac{5}{11}$; $\frac{7}{15}$; $\frac{10}{40}$; $\frac{11}{22}$

Part 2:
1. $\frac{2}{3}$ = R
2. $\frac{3}{5}$ = L
3. $\frac{9}{10}$ = E
4. $\frac{5}{8}$ = F
5. $\frac{1}{2}$ = G
6. $\frac{4}{5}$ = D
7. $\frac{7}{8}$ = I
8. $\frac{5}{7}$ = S
9. $\frac{3}{4}$ = L
10. $\frac{11}{12}$ = O

Sign reads: Grilled Frog Legs

Puzzle 26 (pg 32)
The Magic Number Hat

2.1	0.2	0.8	1.4	1.5
1.3	1.9	2.0	0.1	0.7
0	0.6	1.2	1.8	2.4
1.7	2.3	0.4	0.5	1.1
0.9	1.0	1.6	2.2	0.3

The magic number is 6.0

Puzzle 27 (pg 33)
The Elusive Punch Line

1. 0.51	12. 66.8
2. 0.5	13. 39.41
3. 20.7	14. 52.71
4. 64.479	15. 4.48
5. 20.7	16. 7.77
6. 7.77	17. 39.41
7. 1.86	18. 4.48
8. 6.11	19. 396.2
9. 52.71	20. 7.42
10. 0.51	21. 6.11
11. 396.2	22. 27.74

The punch line is:
It was the chicken's day off.

Puzzle 28 (pg 34)
Hungry for Decimals

Top tier — Product is 3.7908
Second tier — Product is 0.05213
Third tier — Product is 11.583
Fourth tier — Product is 5.94

The worm's path yields a product of 6.318, which is the number on the top right piece of cake.

Puzzle 29 (pg 35)
Underwater Search

Green		
	2) 4.5	4) 4.3
1) 1.05	3) 1.2	5) 4.5

Yellow	
	7) 36
6) 7	8) 0.02

Blue	
	16) 11
9) 7.2	17) 7.2
10) 6.7	18) 16.6
11) 22	19) 18
12) 16.6	20) 1.2
13) 400	21) 0.7
14) 7.2	22) 18
15) 100	

Pink		
	24) 6	26) 5
23) 5.3	25) 0.2	

Orange		
	28) 4.7	30) 2
27) 1.7	29) 0.5	31) 3.6

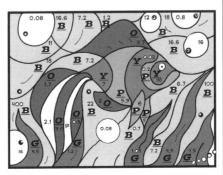

Puzzle 30 (pgs 36–37)
Jigsaw Decimals

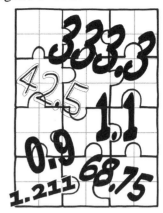

1. 42.5	9. 333.3
2. 68.75	10. NO
3. 0.9	11. 1.1
4. 42.5	12. 333.3
5. 1.1	13. 1.1
6. 42.5	14. 333.3
7. NO	15. 1.2111
8. 68.75	

Puzzle 31 (pg 38)
Canal Conundrum

The correct path is:
A – 2304.36 ....to B – 71.67
to D – 64 ....to G – 7.2079
to F – 935.5 ....to C – 936.38
to E – 88.4.......to the Jolly Cone
Ice Cream Shoppe
Missed intersection–H

Puzzle 32 (pg 39)
The Cover-Up Puzzle

A $6 \times -1 + 7 = 1$
   $4 \times 5 - (-9) = 29$
   $-8 \times (-10) \div (-20) = 4$

B $10 + (-7) - (-25) = 28$
   $2 \times (-2) \times (-5) = 20$
   $(-12) \times (-30) \div (-6) = -60$

   a = 8; b = –16; c = 119

Puzzle 33 (pg 40)
A Puzzle With Pride

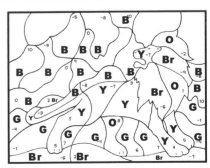

Puzzle 34 (pg 41)
A Strange Bird

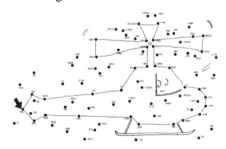

The figure is a helicopter.

Puzzle 35 (pg 42)
Integer Criss-Cross

1. Rule: The top number is the difference between the middle and the bottom numbers. The left number is the divisor, the center is the dividend, the right number is the quotient.

   Missing numbers:

   2nd cross: 18

   3rd cross: −11 on right;
   −308 on bottom

   4th cross: center is −86

2. Rule: The bottom number is the product of the top and the center. The right-hand number is the sum of the left and center numbers.

   Missing numbers:

   2nd cross: −96

   3rd cross: −11

   4th cross: −12 on left;
   −216 on bottom

3. Rule: The bottom number is the quotient of the top and center numbers. The right-hand number is the product of the left and center numbers.

   Missing numbers:

   2nd cross: 204 on right;
   −43 on bottom

   3rd cross: −5 on left;
   −12 in center

   4th cross: −39 on top;
   −13 in center

Puzzle 36 (pg 43)
Escape From the Swamp

Puzzle 37 (pg 44)
Alphabet Soup

1. 10^6 = A
2. 8^3 = N, 2^9 = J
3. 2^3 = H
4. 20^4 = R
5. 5^3 = M
6. 7^3 = I
7. 1^9 = B
8. 15^2 = S
9. 9^3 = C
10. 200^3 = G
11. 4^3 = O, 2^6 = V
12. 3^5 = T
13. 18^2 = L
14. 2^5 = W
15. 160^2 = P
16. 33^2 = E
17. 17^2 = D
18. 5^4 = F

Some possible answers (Things you would not want to find in your soup): frog, spider, owl, inchworm, dirt, screw, ant, bee, fox, worm, bee, leaf, flea, mold, rat, cow

Puzzle 38 (pg 45)
Roots + Radicals Race
There is more than one possible path for each mouse. Check paths to see that they follow descending order in value and that each mouse visits snacks in at least three columns.

Puzzle 39 (pg 46)
Exponential Match-Up

a. x^2
b. x^{16}
c. x^5
d. x^8
e. x^{11}
f. x^{10}
g. x^{12}
h. x^{40}
i. missing answer: x^7
j. x^{15}
k. x^6
l. missing answer: x^3
m. x^9
n. x^{20}
o. missing answer: x
p. missing answer: x^4
q. x^{13}
r. x^{14}

Puzzle 40 (pg 47)
Hidden Proverb

1. 53 (O)
2. 45 (L)
3. 10 (N)
4. 25 (E)
5. y^2 (D)
6. 10 (N)
7. 4 (B)
8. y^7 (T)
9. 45 (L)
10. 10 (N)
11. 200 (I)
12. 53 (O)
13. 125 (P)
14. x^9 (S)
15. 30 (R)
16. 25 (E)
17. 25 (E)
18. x^{20} (W)
19. x^{20} (W)
20. x^6 (K)
21. y^2 (D)
22. 53 (O)
23. 37 (C)
24. 25 (E)
25. 25 (E)
26. 1280 (G)

Proverb is: One broken leg does not slow down a centipede.

Puzzle 41 (pg 48)
Don't Start the Game

1. 82
2. 11, −11
3. 0.1
4. 6
5. 2.2
6. 9, −9
7. 1.5
8. 13
9. −8
10. −15
11. 60, −60

12. 33
13. –2
14. 0.15
15. –11
16. 2
17. 2.2
18. 10, –10
19. 0.01
20. 101
21. 22
22. –6 BINGO
23. 16
24. 8, –7
25. –8
26. 15
27. 6
28. –9

The answers that show up in more than one BINGO square are: 2.2; –8; and 6. You can call BINGO after finding the answer to problem # 22.

Puzzle 42 (pg 49)
Cool Calculations
Across
3. 899
6. 66
7. 307
9. 50
10. 44
12. 111
14. 12
15. 33
Down
1. 19
2. 0
3. 86
4. 93
5. 275
6. 64
8. 141
11. 21
13. 15

Puzzle 43 (pg 50)
Good Advice
1. x = 1 (A)
2. x = 3 (C)
3. y = 20 (T)
4. x = 21 (U)
5. x = 5 (E)
6. n = 2 (B)
7. b = 20 (T)
8. a = 19 (S)
9. p = 20 (T)
10. y = 18 (R)
11. d = 4 (D)
12. g = 19 (S)

13. n = 21 (U)
The missing words are *cat* and *dustbuster*.

Puzzle 44 (pg 51)
A Colorful Character

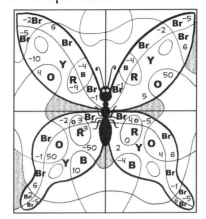

Puzzle 45 (pg 52)
Domino Equations
1. H
2. F
3. M
4. D
5. J
6. G
7. N
8. B or E
9. A
10. I
11. C
12. K
13. E
14. L
15. O

Puzzle 46 (pg 53)
Clockwise Variables
1. y = 180
2. y = –18
3. y = 12
4. x = 3, –3
5. y = 78
6. y = –20
7. y = 142
8. x = 5, –5
9. x = 11, –11
10. y = –12
11. y = 108
12. x = 6, –6

Puzzle 47 (pg 54)
Kernel Computations
Answer to riddle: hot popcorn

Puzzle 48 (pg 55)
Who Gets the Pizza?
1. –12.........(M – Movie Theater)
2. 87..........(I – Insurance Office)
3. 440.........(Y – YMCA)
4. 0.02........(A – Auto Shop)
5. $^7/_{12}$ ....(S – Sweet Shop)
6. 6^3............(M – Market)
7. 45,679....(G – Glass Shop)
8. $2^3/_4$ ....(N – Nursery)
9. 19...........(U – Upholstery)
10. Delivery goes to the gymnasium.

Puzzle 49 (pg 56)
She's Got Clues!
1. 1000 (N)
2. 3210 (I)
3. 25 (P)
4. $1^1/_8$ (T)
5. 6.546 (S)
6. 3220 (R)
7. 25 (P)
8. 6.6 (A)
9. –7 (W)
Clue # 4 is pawprints

Puzzle 50 (pg 57)
Calculations on Target

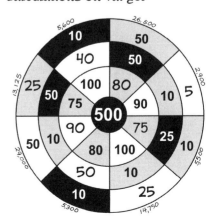